RMS *St Helena*

and the South Atlantic Islands

Robert A. Wilson F.R.S.A.

Whittles Publishing

Published by
Whittles Publishing,
Dunbeath Mains Cottages,
Dunbeath,
Caithness KW6 6EY,
Scotland, UK
www.whittlespublishing.com

© 2006 Robert A. Wilson

ISBN 1-904445-24-1

Typeset by Ailsa M. K. Morrison

Printed by Bell & Bain Ltd., Glasgow

Contents

Foreword

This is an important book for two reasons, for it describes just what a talented radio officer could do in his sometimes lonely role as a one-man department contributing to the running of a happy and efficient ship, and what it was like to be a merchant seaman in the force that liberated the British Falkland Islands in 1982. Military memoirs abound but little has been written, or photographed, about those civilian men and women who suddenly found themselves in a Services environment that went to war.

We can now look back on only eighty years of the Merchant Navy's saga when radio officers were an essential part of a ship's life, whether it was a large passenger liner or a modest-sized tramp ship. Radio officers have been swept away in the relentless progress of communications: they went the same way as telegraphy delivery boys on bicycles. As managers of St Helena's vital shipping service (1977–2001) at their base in a Cornish fishing village, Curnow Shipping had the first ever telex machine in the community which, by 1997, was one of the last of only five in the whole of the county. In 1977 communications with St Helena were only by costly cablegram: by 2001 contact was, as the slogan went, 'at the touch of a button'. There was, as all too often, a human price for this progress and Bob Wilson modestly tells us of how he adapted to it and still remained a cheerful and productive member of the Curnow Shipping team that rendered to a remote and often forgotten British Overseas Territory a high standard of service which, years later, remains a benchmark.

Some of the most graphic parts of this book recount how Bob and his shipmates of Curnow's sea staff were swept into the vortex of a 'Ship Taken Up

From Trade' that made the liberation of the Falklands from Argentinian conquest possible. The acronym STUFT was just how we felt in Curnow Shipping's shore headquarters. It was highly fortuitous that the company was managing G. Rodney-Keene's neat little *Aragonite* at the time. She was rapidly adapted and diverted into St Helena's service, to become nicknamed by the 'Saints' the '12-seater bus', sailing with cargo and 12 passengers 77,000 miles in 16 months of 1982–83. It was also lucky that Blue Funnel SEA were withdrawing their 1964-built *Centaur* from the route for which she had been built, namely Singapore–Western Australia and had become available for charter and possible purchase. Thanks to the stark realisation of the situation by Clive Warren, who looked after St Helena affairs at the Overseas Development Administration, the cost of chartering *Centaur* was extracted from the appropriate budget in Whitehall and thus was provided a newer and larger ship to replace the Old RMS *St Helena*. Because of her many operational failings and an evident lack of care, the option to purchase *Centaur* was not exercised in March 1983, but she did point the way ahead and seven years later the New RMS *St Helena* emerged.

After the Falklands episode was over, Bob chronicles the taunt from some of the sea staff who were not among those who crewed the Old RMS in the Falklands— 'where's the story: you got there after all the action was over'. The story was the outright success of the mothership and the mine-sweeping operation. Because the Argentinian navy had laid a large, uncharted number and wide variety of mines, the two RN mine-hunters were tasked to take 25 weeks to do the job. That it took only five weeks was not only because of the round-the-clock work seven days a week but the objectivity of MoD planning that made *St Helena* with HMS *Ledbury* and HMS *Brecon* self-sustained and independent of everything else that was going on. In the Old RMS's subsequent service (October 1982–May 1983) running on the supply line of personnel between Ascension and Stanley, the ship was always the first choice ahead of the other two on the route, namely *Uganda* and *St Edmund*, on which to travel because the Curnow way of doing things was to treat all the passengers equally.

Bob Wilson is typically modest about his contribution to the ships he sailed on and the company for which he worked. Few radio officers in modern times played such a comprehensive role in the ship's life. This ranged from keeping anchor watches in the Falklands to giving inspiring lectures to passengers about the days of sail that, in their content, captured some of the terror of big sailing ships in bad weather. His talent for taking a good picture is for all to wonder at within the covers of this book. Bob says little of his craftsmanship that has made him one of the world's leading miniature ship model makers — truly an equal of the master builder of all time, Donald McNarry. It was a visual pleasure which was the result of my persuading Baxter Associates, who coordinated and designed the whole of the New RMS's interior, to include an area in the main foyer where the Wilson Collection of historic ships associated with St Helena were displayed from 1990 until Andrew Weir Shipping disposed of them in 2005. Not least of all were Bob's talents in doing his primary job of keeping communications open with Curnow's main office, never more so than during the engine room fire on the original *St Helena* in 1985 and the rescue of the last survivor from *Oman Sea One*. It was an immeasurable comfort and reassurance that, back in Cornwall, we knew what was going on all the time and were thus placed in a position to relay the news to friends, relations, underwriters and principals.

Looking back on the 25-year history of Curnow Shipping there was always an aura of Camelot about it, from its lucky beginnings, winning a government tender three times through to the company's self-destructed ending. For one brief moment it was all that many a proud, established British shipping line had been from Port Line to Blue Funnel, from Union Castle to Shaw Savill, all of whom are now fading into history. Perhaps the proudest and most enduring legacy, one in which Bob played a significant part, was getting the Saints to sea on their own ship and some of them onward into international careers in shipping.

We can thank and salute Bob Wilson and his publisher for recording something that is more than a footnote to the maritime history of Britain.

Andrew M. B. Bell OBE RD
Managing Director
Curnow Shipping 1977–2000

Chapter 1

RMS *St Helena* — an Indian Summer

Late one January evening in 1979, I was taking a quiet drink in the officers' lounge of the cargo liner *Bandama* as we sailed through a hot and sultry night off the coast of West Africa. That night I received a telephone call that was to change my entire life from that moment on. It was to take me back to a lifestyle that I thought had gone forever and lead me into numerous adventures, some pleasant, some unpleasant, which were beyond my wildest imaginings!

We had just spent over a month loading logs in the West African ports of Abidjan and San Pedro. It was good to get to sea again and we all looked forward to leaving the hot, sultry African coastal waters for the fresher and cooler climes of the Mediterranean. I was not unhappy with my position as radio officer in the *Bandama*. She was a new ship, less than two years old, and reasonably comfortable. The run, however, was boring in the extreme with weeks spent loading logs in the West African rivers with little or no chance to get ashore.

I had been at sea for eighteen years and had progressed from general cargo ships, colliers and iron ore carriers to the prestigious liners of the Union-Castle Mail Steamship Company. By 1974 I was senior radio officer in the cargo passenger liner *Good Hope Castle* on the UK–South Africa run, calling at the Atlantic islands of Ascension and St Helena. Life in the *Good Hope Castle* seemed perfect, but after two years the company decided to 'get out of shipping'. Rather than wait for redundancy, I resigned and joined the British shipping

1

company Silver Line. I had been very well treated and between 1976 and 1979 had travelled extensively in three different ships, visiting the Philippines, Japan, Canada, the USA, Australia, Mexico, Saudi Arabia, Suez, Mediterranean ports and West Africa. Life, however, was beginning to pall and I longed for the happy days of the passenger liners that I believed had gone for ever.

At about 2100 hours, the telephone rang: it was the third officer on the bridge. He informed me that he was talking to a small passenger liner on the VHF radiotelephone. The ship was the RMS *St Helena*, en route from the islands of St Helena and Ascension towards Las Palmas and Avonmouth. There was someone aboard who wished to speak to me. On arrival on the bridge I was pleasantly surprised to find former shipmate Colin Dellar on the telephone. We had first sailed together in 1965 when I was 4th radio officer in the passenger liner *Windsor Castle* and he was assistant purser. We had subsequently sailed together again in 1972 in the *Pendennis Castle*, by which time I was 2nd radio officer and Colin was purser.

He told me that after the demise of the Union-Castle Line they had all been made redundant. The mail contract was then awarded to the small British management company Curnow Shipping, which operated from a small cottage in Helston, Cornwall. They had obtained a small 3,150 gross ton Canadian coaster called the *Northland Prince*. The ship had carried passengers on the Canadian coast between 1963 and the late 1970s when she was withdrawn from service and laid up in Vancouver. She had been brought across to Southampton and refitted as a Class I passenger ship suitable to carry seventy-six passengers on international voyages and renamed *St Helena*. A number of old friends from Union-Castle were serving aboard, these included chief engineers Bryan Gillott and Bryan Cooper, and pursers Geoff Shallcross, Jeannie Bonner and 'Dusty' Miller. There were also a number of other ex Union-Castle staff aboard whom I did not know. Colin advised me that the ship had just completed her first two or three voyages and was now settling down well. He then asked if I was interested in the position of radio officer—they were operating a voyage on, voyage off leave system and so far had only one permanent radio officer. I made a snap decision there and then and said that I would love to join. Next, I spoke to Captain Wyatt who told me that he would telephone Andrew Bell, the Managing Director, that night and see what could be arranged.

The following morning, the chief engineer looked in at the radio office and told me that the *St Helena* was on the telephone again. Colin confirmed that Captain Wyatt had spoken to Mr Bell and that everything was fine and I would be employed on his recommendation. As soon as I went off watch, I went down to offer my resignation to Captain Tuddenham. He was quite horrified and

The Northland Prince
(courtesy of the Donald Murray Collection of the Vancouver Maritime Museum)

said that I was being rather hasty, leaving the security of a company with over sixty ships to join a precarious and unknown venture that would probably fizzle out after two or three voyages. I would not be moved, however, and he reluctantly accepted my resignation. Years later, I was reminded of his words when I saw him on TV in command of the bulk carrier in which Michael Palin sailed during his *Round the World in Eighty Days* film. Silver Line by that time was long gone, but I was still sailing in the *St Helena*!

On our arrival at Sete on the Mediterranean coast of France, I signed off the *Bandama* and flew home only to find that I had missed the *St Helena* by a few days and she had sailed south again on voyage six. I met with Andrew Bell in London and was duly taken on by Curnow Shipping.

One month and sixteen days after leaving the *Bandama*, I joined the *St Helena* in Avonmouth, Bristol. As the taxi approached the ship, I was surprised how tiny she looked. Although smart and well painted, she nevertheless had a

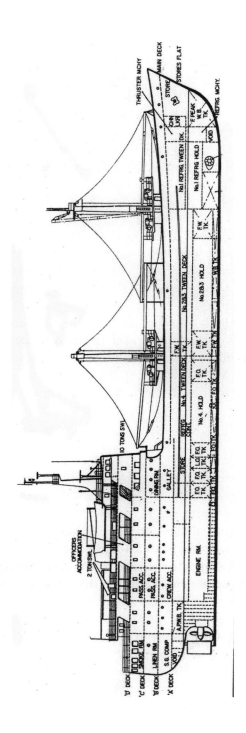

St Helena's *profile plan.*
(courtesy of 'The Motor Ship)

slightly battered appearance. The heavy steel bulwarks were badly twisted and distorted in places, although the main hull plating looked smooth enough. She also had a slight list, as if leaning on the quay for support. At the top of the gangway, I found myself entering the forward lounge that ran almost the full breadth of the ship. Sounds of sporadic laughter were coming from the purser's cabin on the port side. The small room was quite full, and I was delighted to find that I knew most of them: it was like a nautical homecoming. Most were old shipmates from Union-Castle and the remainder of the officers came from Ocean Fleets, Blue Star, Shell Tankers, New Zealand Shipping, Silver Line, Buries Markes, Shaw Savill, P&O and the Royal Fleet Auxiliary, all once well-known companies. The crew were all recruited from the island of St Helena and were collectively known as 'Saints'. They were totally different from the Filipinos with whom I had sailed in Silver Line. The Saints, although they came in all colours from white to black were British, the island of St Helena being a British colony—pro-British, English speaking and enjoying a less hectic pace of life. The islanders were peaceful and law-abiding with a friendly and gentle disposition and made an ideal crew for the little ship.

Despite the age of the ship, the accommodation was quite adequate, although not luxurious. All our cabins were similar and all the officers except the assistant catering officer and chef had their own cabins complete with bathrooms. (Initially, the chef and assistant catering officer had to share a double berth cabin, but this was rectified in due course.) The captain's cabin was fairly large and had a small sleeping area curtained off from the main cabin. The chief engineer had a larger cabin than the captain, but without the curtained-off sleeping area.

I was pleased to find that I was accommodated on the bridge deck adjacent to the radio office. The tiny radio office itself had more sophisticated equipment crammed into it than any other ship I had sailed in. Although the big passenger liners had doubled up equipment, none had teleprinters. The *St Helena* did, but I looked on it with some suspicion—I did not feel it was really necessary on such a small vessel, but it was there, so I would have to live with it. Prior to joining, I had attended a teleprinter course at the STC factory, which was quite thorough as far as the working and repair of the equipment was concerned. But those of us attending wanted to know how to use a teleprinter to send and receive messages more than how it worked or how to repair it, and none of the technicians was able to help us as far as that was concerned. The radio officer with whom I was to share the ship, Neil Abbott, an amiable New Zealander, explained that the teleprinter had only been installed on the previous voyage. He had encountered the same problems but was able to give me a quick run through on how to use it before going on leave.

On sailing, I conducted our initial communications in Morse code as I had always done. The first evening at sea we were in the traffic list at Portishead Radio and again I received the message in the traditional manner using Morse. Next morning, Captain Wyatt came along to the radio office with a telex message. On that particular voyage his wife and two young sons were sailing with us and he had brought the boys along to watch a telex message being sent! How I wished I had made my first attempt the previous night in privacy. With an outward show of calm confidence, I tuned the transmitter in on the appropriate frequency for Land's End Radio. I then set the digital receiver to the correct frequency. All was silent apart from the odd crackle and hiss from the receiver. Uttering a silent prayer, I pressed the call button on the control unit. The cricket-like pulsing sound commenced immediately and after about five seconds, a row of lights flashed on the control unit and the whirr of the teleprinter daisy wheel commenced. I pressed the 'Who are you?' button on the keyboard and within seconds Land's End Radio's answerback typed itself out on the machine. I replied with our answerback and typed in 'Good morning, please connect with 45654 Curnow G.' 'Good morning,' it replied, 'please wait!' After a few seconds, the machine typed 'Go ahead!' I again pressed the 'Who are you?' button and '45654 Curnow G' came back. All I had to do then was

St Helena*'s radio office (with the author)*

press the 'Send' button and the punched paper tape began to chatter through the machine and a copy of the message was simultaneously printed in the Curnow office and on the ship's teleprinter. So, after eighteen years at sea, I had made my last communication with Portishead Radio using Morse code. Morse was not dead, however, it remained in common use right until the day I left the sea thirteen years later. The captain and his two sons departed as impressed as I was with the ease of telex.

The advent of telex, although it made the actual sending and receiving of messages considerably easier did not reduce the workload. Telex was charged by time and not by the number of words. One minute of telex cost only fifty pence in 1979 and quite a number of words could be sent in that time. So, as communications became cheaper and easier, the size and frequency of messages initially doubled. Within a few years it multiplied a hundredfold. That this was happening on a universal basis became obvious by the fact that the telex channels were always busy no matter how many more were added. Time once consumed by sending messages in Morse code was replaced by typing lengthy messages onto punched tape and then waiting, sometimes for hours, for a vacant channel. Long-distance telephone calls were also on the increase.

For my first two weeks aboard the ship, I was hard pressed to keep up although at the same time I was supremely happy. Life was made more satisfactory because I was back with old friends. The old ship was running like a sewing machine and I was surprised that there was practically no vibration in the main parts of the accommodation. Only the stern gallery, directly above the propeller was subject to a continuous, undulating rumble and heave as the small ship breasted the swells. The food, cooked under the watchful eye of Joe Laight, former head chef of the liner *Windsor Castle*, was plain, but wholesome.

Discipline was relaxed and there was no master-at-arms to watch our every move. The passengers had the run of the ship and the foredeck was used for deck sports, deck quoits and sunbathing. A big round swimming pool which had once been a storage tank was also placed on the foredeck and filled every day. It was always popular with passengers and officers. The crew were allowed to use it as well at certain times in the evenings. Senior crew members comprising the bosun and bosun's mate, assistant cook, baker and engine-room storekeeper could all use the passenger facilities and public rooms provided they were correctly dressed in uniform. This was the first time I had come across that privilege and it was never abused, but the only time they ever seemed to make use of it was on fancy dress evenings or other special occasions.

With a general decline in passenger ships, press broadcasts had ceased and I no longer had the time-consuming task of receiving long press broadcasts every night in Morse code as had been the custom in the Union-Castle Line. The ship's company was simply kept informed of what was going on by means of the World News followed by News About Britain being piped through the public rooms at 1800 each evening. A daily information sheet was also typed by the assistant purser.

The layout of the ship was very simple. The lowest deck housed the crew and galley and crew messroom, which doubled as their recreation room. The next deck up had sixteen passenger cabins numbering one to twelve and fourteen to seventeen—there was no cabin thirteen in keeping with seafaring and other superstitions—which berthed between one and three people each. At the after end was a double-berth cabin for our two stewardesses, Glenda and Maureen, and also a self-service laundry for the use of passengers, officers and stewardesses. At the after end of the engine casing was a small but well-provided shop for the use of all on board. This was presided over by our assistant pursers, Angie or Jeannie. At the forward end was the dining saloon for the passengers and officers, with a pantry centrally placed. It came as a great relief to me when I was advised that the 'privilege' of a passenger table had been rescinded as far as the radio officers were concerned: no reason was given and I didn't ask in case it might be reinstated! (I was less pleased that first class rail travel was also rescinded!) Two sittings were normally held for each meal: the first sitting including the junior officers on a long table separate from the passengers, at second sitting the captain, chief officer, chief engineer, purser and surgeon all had passenger tables. The long officers' table at second sitting was occupied by the purser catering, assistant purser, radio officer and electrical officer.

The next deck had the main lounge and bar at the forward end and the stern gallery at the after end. Thirteen passenger cabins were situated between the lounges on this deck. Also the purser and catering officer were accommodated at the forward end, aft of the main lounge. A small office was provided aft of the lounge on the port side. This was shared by purser, assistant purser and catering officer.

Above this level was the accommodation for the bulk of the officers, the consulting room, hospital and officers' lounge/bar. The officers' lounge/bar was a very small room which was seldom used. When I had first gone to sea, officers' bars did not exist in any of my earlier ships. They were not really necessary in the big passenger ships as we could either drink in our cabins or use the passenger bars. The officers' bar quickly fell into disuse and was eventually converted into a very comfortable 'quiet lounge' for the use of passengers or officers.

Soon after I joined, the chief engineer's office, which was situated next to the quiet lounge was then converted into a cabin for the second catering officer, leaving the chef as sole occupant of the original shared cabin. At the same time, a small storeroom just aft of the main lounge was converted into the chief engineer's office. This was fitted by a 'stable' type door, the top half of which was usually left open when the chief was in the office. Passengers passing the office at various times of the day would often stop for a chat with the chief, which added to the general friendliness of the ship. Relations between officers, crew and passengers on the old *St Helena* were far superior to anything I had come across previously, or indeed, anything that came after.

Over the next eleven years, the *St Helena* was to make seventy-one voyages of which I completed thirty-five! Although I expected to enjoy a voyage on, voyage off leave system, this was not to commence immediately. I was told that I would first have to complete two consecutive voyages in order to get accustomed to the ship. In actual fact, I was accustomed to it within the first couple of weeks!

Our first port of call was Las Palmas, in the Canary Islands: this leg of the voyage took about five days. In winter, we would often encounter bad weather between Land's End and Cape Finisterre, during which we would see little of the passengers apart from at meal times. By the time we passed Lisbon, the weather was usually on the mend with sparkling blue sea and sky. Arrival at Las Palmas was generally about breakfast time with departure set for late afternoon. The main purpose of the stay was to take on fuel and fresh stores for the next leg of the voyage. After leaving Las Palmas, we were all able to settle down to the seven-day run to Ascension Island—this was regarded by most people as the best part of all. The weather was always stable and calm, although prone to heavy rain off West Africa during certain months. The passengers enjoyed a carefree, lazy existence as we sailed south. The older ones would usually sit inside the main lounge in a long row beneath the forward windows talking, reading, knitting or just dozing. Others would prefer to sit on the promenade decks, out of the blazing sun, but still in the open air. The children and younger passengers enjoyed the circular swimming pool on the foredeck, while others lay around on the boat deck sunbathing. Afternoons were generally regarded as the 'quiet time', although on my first voyage this was not the case. We carried a record number of twenty-five children whose boisterous laughter made itself felt throughout the ship, and added to the general feeling of happiness on board.

Deck sports were often held on the foredeck during the late afternoons and these included tug of wars, wheelbarrow races, egg and spoon races, sack races, cricket and a whole host of other activities suited to the deck of a small ship. There was a very warm family feeling to it all and it added to the domestic scene to see our stewardesses Glenda and Maureen hoovering down the carpets before breakfast each day. Both these charming ladies remained at sea for many years, both rising to the rank of second catering officer in the early 1990s.

After the evening meal, most people took coffee and liqueurs in the stern gallery before moving to the forward lounge for the evening's entertainment. This followed the same pattern as in the Union-Castle liners. There was frog racing, where five flat wooden frogs with a long string passed through their centres were propped against a 'starting board'. The participants sat in chairs on the other side of the lounge facing the frogs. At the order to start, they would all begin pulling or jerking the strings in order to make the frog move towards them. The purser declared the winner as the first frog which crossed the aluminium strip separating the small dance floor from the carpet. Before each race a tote was open and passengers and officers could place small bets in units of ten pence on the frog of their choice. Some passengers would bet as much as five pounds on a frog, but it was hard to predict who would win. There were no heavy winners or losers and it was all a good bit of fun in which the profits were always donated to various charities. There were table quizzes, charades, tombola, dances, drawing games, fancy dress evenings and even pyjama parties. Modern films were also shown every few days on a 16 mm movie projector set up in the lounge. Twice a voyage I would put on a full evening's entertainment in the main lounge in the form of an illustrated slide show showing the gradual transition from sail to steam in the Merchant Navy over the last hundred years or so. Much to our initial surprise, these talks became extremely popular and were always well attended. I realised early on that the passengers were not really interested in technicalities, but salty sea stories. They loved sitting in comfort as the ship traversed the tropics, watching images of long-dead seamen battling the elements in hard-pressed square riggers off Cape Horn, or living again the dramatic and adventurous lives of famous, and not-so-famous, merchant seamen of years gone by. We also had dance and cabaret evenings and the ever-popular barbeque on deck. The main feature of the barbeque was a huge side of beef which was traditionally called 'a steamboat round'. It took all day to cook and was carved on deck as required by whoever was chef at the time. There were also steaks, chicken, pork, sausages, jacket potatoes and mounds of salads and sweets. During these barbeques there was also dancing on deck beneath a million stars in the crystal clear nights off the African coast.

As we crossed the equator, there was always a 'Crossing the Line' ceremony, where a number of victims were brought before King Neptune, his Queen and court officials. The captain and chief engineer, heavily made up, usually took the part of King and Queen. The catering officer, dressed in a ragged tail coat, was master of ceremonies and called loudly for each victim to be dragged forth to be accused of some crime. A typical accusation reserved for the best looking young lady victim ran something like this, 'You have been brought before His Majesty King Neptune on the charge that, on the previous evening, with malice and aforethought, you ran through the main passenger lounge wearing only three small beads. Two of these beads, I might add, were beads of sweat! How plead ye, guilty or very guilty?' 'Very guilty!' roars the King and Queen, backed up by the onlookers. 'Take her away!' She was then deposited on a table covered by a large sheet liberally stained with tomato ketchup. The purser, dressed as a surgeon, then rubbed the victim down with a kipper as she lay face down on the table. An egg was then stuffed up each side of the lower half of the swimming costume, which was actually a one piece type over a bikini. The eggs were then ceremonially broken with a big hammer. Another sheet was placed on top and the purser leapt beneath it. After loud shouts, much wriggling and giggling, the purser emerged with the one-piece swimming costume, whirling it round his head and discarding it. The young lady, still wrapped in the sheet was carried across to the barber, normally the 2nd engineer. He proceeded to shave the victim with a huge wooden razor and then she was covered in custard pies, boxes of chocolate ice cream, flour and cocoa powder until she was just a shapeless mess. She was then taken up to the top of the pool steps and, after the sheet was removed, thrown in where the two 'bears' quickly rescued her and assisted with the removal of the goo. She emerged clean and bikini-clad, to present King and Queen with a bow of thanks for their 'leniency'. The victims were all chosen beforehand, so none of the onlookers had any fear of taking part if they did not wish. Once the ceremony was complete, the officials and victims were invited to the captain's cabin for a drink before lunch.

The next port of call was Ascension Island, where we usually anchored for a day in order to work cargo. On my first call in the *St Helena*, a group of officers were invited ashore to a garden party at the administrator's residence. Dressed in our best white uniforms, we embarked in the launch. As we headed for the shore, I saw for the first time what a peculiar looking ship the *St Helena* was. The funnel was so short that it was not visible over the lifeboats. The white hull paint came far too low and was almost touching the water at the stern. The green hull paint at the forward end was much more in evidence and gave the ship a strange look. Nevertheless, it didn't bother me at all, I had found a very happy ship and was completely content. The party was a dignified affair with the Union Flag flying from the flagstaff and everyone behaving very properly. Returning to the ship, we found things very crowded. In addition to our seventy-six cabin passengers, we had embarked a further forty-eight deck passengers for St Helena. These were workers returning home on leave and were hence in high spirits. Ascension Island did not have a permanent population: everyone there was either working, or the family of someone who was working there. The main employers were Cable & Wireless, BBC, NASA and the American Air Base. The workforce was obtained mainly from St Helena. The distance between the two islands was about 700 miles and the passage time approximately 48 hours. The deck passengers were allowed to use the stern gallery lounge (the cabin passengers being confined to the main lounge for this part of the voyage), but had to sleep dormitory style on the boat deck which had canvas screens laced round the sides while they were aboard. During the day, this was quite bright because as well as flexible plastic windows being included in the screens, the corrugated plastic covering above was translucent. Generally, they had become very Americanised and were great enthusiasts of Country and Western music which they played all day and well into the night. The bar in the main lounge was available to them via an open side window and this became very busy. It was not unusual for a grinning deck passenger to arrive and order pints of beer by the dozen. Naturally enough, with more than 120 people on board, they could not all be fed at once. Three sittings were provided for all meals until we arrived at our destination. We had always had deck passengers in the *Good Hope Castle*, my last Union-Castle liner. There, they were all confined to the dormitory on the bridge deck, where they also ate, but the *Good Hope Castle* had been more than five times the size of the *St Helena* and they were easily absorbed, simply because of the size of the vessel. It was as if the clock had been turned back more than a century and we were on a far-eastern passenger steamer reminiscent of the days of Joseph Conrad. It was always with some relief that we arrived at the anchorage in James' Bay St Helena and the noisy, but happy crowd disembarked. Once they had gone, the cabin passengers, even the ones en route to Cape Town, also disembarked to various hotels. Because of the difficulties of going ashore by launch, especially if there was a high swell running, elderly or less nimble passengers were disembarked by cargo box. It was lowered on deck by one of the ship's derricks and the passengers would be lifted into it. An officer or member of staff would always accompany them to allay any fears. The box was then hoisted into a barge and taken in to the wharf where the shore crane would lift it ashore. On my first voyage the passenger box was a small, scruffy affair; it was quickly replaced by a more substantial aluminium cage-type box with open sides. A quiet calm then descended on the ship and everyone set about getting it ready for the next lot of passengers as the cargo for the island was disembarked into huge barges and lighters that lay alongside. St Helena, as Ascension, did not have a jetty suitable for big or even small ships, so we always had to anchor off.

The island of St Helena was the main reason for the existence of the ship St

Helena. In the days of sail, it had been an important staging post for ships outward bound to the east via the Cape of Good Hope. In the early nineteenth century, it had been a place of exile for the Emperor Napoleon after his final defeat at Waterloo. With the opening of the Suez Canal in 1869, St Helena was used much less often by ships as they were no longer forced to sail around Good Hope on their way to the East. Being a British colony, however, it still had to be maintained. Supplies at that time were carried regularly from Britain and South Africa in ships of the Union Line and the Castle Line. These two British companies shared the contract to carry Royal Mail between the UK and South Africa in their small passenger steamers. It was a condition of the mail contract that the ships were to call regularly at the island with supplies.

At the turn of the century, both these companies merged to form what was to become the famous Union-Castle Mail Steamship Company. They ran three distinct sections, the largest part of which was the South African Mail Service. Their biggest and fastest ships ran between Britain and South Africa, running along the South African coast as far as Durban, before returning the same way. They did not call at St Helena. A secondary service of smaller 'intermediate' liners ran round Africa via the Suez Canal and called at St Helena each voyage. The third section of the company was concerned only with a small number of cargo ships which were employed on worldwide trading.

A British garrison had been maintained on the island until about 1906 and its withdrawal was something of a blow to the island. It was still a British Colony, though, and still had to be supplied by a regular steamer service and so the Union-Castle intermediates continued to call at the island. The rapid increase in the popularity of air travel in the 1960s did not change things at all: St Helena had no airstrip and was not likely to get one in the foreseeable future. When the Suez Canal was closed in the Suez crisis of 1967, it spelt the death knell for the Union-Castle Round Africa Service and the intermediate liners were all disposed of, leaving only the large passenger mail ships. About that time, the Mail Service had been speeded up and the ships were running at a service speed of 22.5 knots, sailing between Britain and Cape Town in eleven and a half days. Although the three most modern liners, *Transvaal Castle*, *Windsor Castle* and *Pendennis Castle* were capable of much higher speeds, the older ships were not and calls at St Helena could not be fitted into the speeded up schedule. With the disposal of the intermediates, a stopgap solution was made to supply the island. This involved using the old *Capetown Castle* on a separate but slower run between Britain and South Africa which allowed for calls at St Helena. The Mail Service was maintained by the three newest liners mentioned above plus the older *Edinburgh Castle* and *Pretoria Castle* and two brand new cargo mail ships, *Good Hope Castle* and *Southampton*

Castle which had replaced the old *Athlone Castle* and *Stirling Castle* in 1965. These seven ships did not call at St Helena simply because *Edinburgh Castle* and *Pretoria Castle* were pushed to the limit at the new service speed of 22.5 knots and a Mail Service of one ship per week had to be maintained from Britain and South Africa.

On the withdrawal of the thirty-year old *Capetown Castle* in 1967, the problem of St Helena arose once more. The problem was solved by fitting the *Good Hope Castle* and *Southampton Castle* with accommodation for twelve cabin passengers plus forty-eight deck passengers each. When this was completed, both ships returned to the Mail Service running at an increased service speed of 23.5 knots. This allowed them to include Ascension Island and St Helena in the normal mail schedule without upsetting any of the arrival times in either Britain or South Africa.

This new service continued until 1978 when the Union-Castle Line withdrew all seven mail ships in preparation for getting out of shipping altogether. For a while, St Helena was left to fend for itself. Fortunately, owing to the foresight of Andrew Bell, the tiny *Northland Prince* was found in Vancouver and refitted under her new name of *St Helena* to carry on an abbreviated Mail Service running between Avonmouth in the UK to the Canary Islands, Ascension Island, St Helena and Cape Town.

Although I had been to St Helena many times before in the *Good Hope Castle*, I had only been ashore once, and then only for about two hours. The *St Helena* was scheduled for a three-day call, and so I was able to get ashore under more leisurely circumstances. Island tours were provided for passengers in a ramshackle island bus and I was able to join one of these for a good look round the island. We had lunch in the courtyard of the Consulate Hotel, Jamestown. This consisted of a simple, but good meal of fish and chips washed down by several cans of beer. Walking back through the seafront archway to the wharf, I noticed a red rusty piece of machinery sticking from the sea several hundred feet out. After making some enquiries, I was told that it was the wreck of the Victorian steamship *Papanui*, which came in on fire in 1911. Always having had a keen interest in nautical history and wrecks, I quickly unearthed the following story.

The *Papanui* had been built by Denny, of Dumbarton, Scotland in 1898 for the New Zealand Shipping Company. She was a steel-hulled passenger liner of 6,372 gross tons with a length of 430 feet and a breadth of 54 feet. In addition to a large number of passengers, she could carry 100,000 frozen sheep carcasses as well as general cargo. She was fitted with two tall masts and originally carried a fair amount of sail, both square, and fore-and-aft. A number of years after her launch, she was sold to an Australian consortium and whilst she retained the name *Papanui*, the port of registry was changed from London to Melbourne.

On the evening of August 19th, 1911, the *Papanui* sailed from Tilbury and the ship sailed for Las Palmas, en route to Australia via the Cape. On arrival at Las Palmas, the ship took on fresh water and bunker coal. The coaling operation took most of the day and the ship was black from stem to stern as the coal was very dry and dusty. On the 3rd September, a fire broke out in the coal bunkers, but the passengers were advised that this had been extinguished promptly. Fire again broke out on the 5th September and although every effort was made to conceal this from the passengers, the smoke and fumes made it obvious. The efforts of officers and crew to put out the fire were continuous and strenuous. As the ship crossed the Equator, the fire was again contained, but not extinguished. By the 8th September, the fire again began to make its presence felt. The ship was, at this time, still heading for Cape Town despite pleas to the captain to put in to St Helena. Eventually the *Papanui*, now trailing a long plume of smoke, altered course towards the island. Shortly afterwards she again altered towards the Cape. This happened three times before Mr Birkett, the chief officer, finally persuaded the captain to put in to St Helena.

The following day, the burning *Papanui* nosed into the anchorage and at 1600 hours the anchor thundered to the bottom of James Bay, for all time. During the next six hours the officers and crew of the *Papanui*, aided by the officers and crew of the cable ship *Britannia*, which lay at anchor nearby, fought the fire. This proved an impossible task. At 2245 hours an explosion occurred which blew one of the hatches off. Flames began to pour out of the hold and from that moment onwards *Papanui* was doomed. Almost all of the 500 souls on board were then evacuated. After a further series of explosions, the *Papanui*

The burning Papanui

Papanui *steering gear*

settled on the bottom, although a large amount of the blackened and twisted hull remained above the water. The survivors of the *Papanui* remained on the island for several weeks before being taken off by a New Zealand Shipping company liner diverted for the purpose.

The bulk of the wreck remained visible for several years, but has since settled so that only the top of the steering gear can be seen above water. For diving or snorkelling enthusiasts, there is still quite a lot to see of the wreck in the crystal clear waters of James Bay. The boilers, engines, winches, anchors and cable can be clearly identified. The side plating has collapsed outwards, giving an unimpeded view of the remains.

Over the next few years, we often went out to the wreck site in a boat and, tying up to the steering gear, were able to snorkel over the remains of what was once a very fine example of a Victorian passenger liner.

Several voyages after I joined the *St Helena*, we carried Mr Richard Robbins out to the island. He was the last survivor of the *Papanui*. He was ten years old at the time of the wreck, but he remembered everything clearly and was still extremely fit and active. The above report has been compiled from the official letter which was written to the Governor of St Helena in 1911 by Fred and Frank Ellis, passengers on the *Papanui*

Richard Robbins, the last survivor of the Papanui

16

and also from the personal re-collections of Richard Robbins.

On completion of our cargo discharge, a new lot of passengers embarked and we set off north again to Ascension, leaving all our 'through' passengers in hotels on St Helena. Back at Ascension, all passengers disembarked and we often remained at anchor overnight. These overnight

The plaque given by the Papanui *survivors*

stays were very popular. With no passengers on board, a barbeque was usually held on deck and all the ship's company attended. On these occasions there was no demarcation between officers and crew, we all sat together round tables beneath the awnings eating, drinking and socialising—a far cry from my sea experiences of earlier years.

More passengers were then embarked and conveyed to St Helena, after which we picked up our 'through' passengers and continued on towards the Cape. This leg of the voyage was less predictable as far as the weather was concerned, but it was only occasionally that we encountered anything particularly bad. We normally arrived at Cape Town five or six days after leaving St Helena. All passengers disembarked on arrival and the ship commenced cargo—this would take between three and seven days to complete. It was wonderful to be back in Cape Town after two years' absence, and see again the beautiful city and the majestic Table Mountain beyond. The two years spent in Silver Line when I felt that I had nothing further to look forward to had passed as the summer clouds pass.

There was plenty to do in Cape Town when off duty and we often hired cars and travelled up the coast, or spent the day on the beach or at the seaside resorts which abounded around the coast. In the fourteen years since my first call at the Cape, the city had become practically international. Men and women of all colours and races seemed to get on well together and this was very noticeable in the big hotels or at the swimming pool at Seapoint where the colour bar seemed to have been unofficially abandoned without any undue problems.

The voyage back to Avonmouth was faster. In the early years we did not do a northbound shuttle, but simply called at St Helena, Ascension, Las Palmas and finally Avonmouth. After a number of voyages, Santa Cruz, Tenerife was substituted for Las Palmas. The change was made for operational considerations but it proved popular. We berthed close to the town and, being a seaside resort, it was far more popular with our passengers.

As my second voyage drew to a close, we were advised to proceed to Southampton for our annual dry-dock. When the pilot boarded I was pleased to recognise him as Sam Foulks, who had been chief officer of the old cargo ship *Richmond Castle* which I had sailed in fourteen years previously. We recognised each other immediately and recalled old times as we proceeded to the dry-dock.

It was during this docking that the ship was fitted with a conical funnel extension, which improved the looks of the ship considerably. The level of the green hull paint was also raised, making a further improvement. Shortly after we arrived, the *Queen Elizabeth 2* berthed close to the dry dock. We knew a number of the officers from our Union-Castle days and I made my first visit to the ship. On subsequent evenings they visited us and although we were tiny compared with their ship, several of them indicated that they would love to change places. On completion of the dry dock, we sailed round to Avonmouth to load cargo. At the end of this time I went home for my first leave from the ship.

During my time in Union-Castle, the big passenger liners all had the prefix 'RMS' or 'RMMV' before their names. The former signified 'Royal Mail Steamer' and the latter 'Royal Mail Motor Vessel'. RMS ships could be of any company, provided they carried Royal Mail among their cargo. In the mid 1960s most of the big passenger liners of the major companies carried Royal Mail and therefore carried these prestigious prefixes. Because they were so common, not a great store was put on the title and the ships were usually referred to by their names only. When the great decline in mail ships came, it suddenly seemed to become more important. The *St Helena* therefore made a great show of being RMS *St Helena*. Strictly speaking, as *St Helena* was a motor vessel, the designation should have been 'RMMV', nevertheless she was referred to as 'RMS' for the rest of her days.

The prestige afforded to mail ships may be illustrated by a story of the old Union Line, which carried the mails to South Africa before the amalgamation of Union Line and Castle Line that took place in about 1900 forming the Union-Castle Mail Steamship Company. The story goes that a 500-ton mail ship, with a handful of passengers, a cargo of coal and the Royal Mail aboard, was proceeding down the English Channel when it encountered the British Fleet on manoeuvres. As the small ship approached the great rows of battleships, a hoist of signal flags shot up to the flagship's yardarm declaring 'You are impeding fleet manoeuvres!' The reply from the diminutive ship was short and to the point: 'You are impeding Her Majesty's Mail'! The fleet, before which the world trembled, graciously opened out and the tiny mail ship sailed on, unimpeded!

As time went by, the company was beginning to manage more ships. They already manned the *Celtic Pilot* (formerly *Pentire*) when I joined, but another one had been added. This one was the *St Anne of Alderney*. Part way into my leave, I was sent off to Portsmouth as company representative during the radio survey of the ship, which was too small to carry a radio officer. Here I met Captain Martin Smith who was to be a shipmate for many years to come. Also the engineering superintendent, David Brock, with whom I would liaise over radio matters. The survey went off well and in the evening Captain Smith, Mr Brock and I were invited to dinner with one of the owners of the ship and his wife.

The three captains employed by the company were totally different in age and character. The senior captain was Martin Smith, who had served his time in the Elder Dempster section of Ocean Fleets (formerly Blue Funnel Line). Ironically, he had not been at sea as long as the other two. Absolutely dedicated to life at sea and with a strong interest in square rigged sail and yachting, I found him quite easy to get along with, possibly because of a shared interest in traditional deep water sailing ships. Second in seniority came Captain Bob Wyatt, who had served his time in Clan Line and Union-Castle before graduating to Trinder Anderson and then Bibby Line, in which he rose to command the container ship *Dart America*, sailing out of Southampton. Again, he was easy to get on with and over the years we became firm friends and even now remain in touch. Earlier in his career, he had sailed with Martin Smith in Elder Dempster and it was there that they both met Andrew Bell, Curnow's Managing Director, an association which led them both to Curnow Shipping. Lastly came Captain Paddy Dodkins. Although the junior captain in Curnow Shipping, he was the oldest and certainly most experienced by a number of years. In the late 1950s he had been chief officer in the Blue Funnel liner in which Andrew Bell made his first voyage as a deck apprentice. He normally commanded the *Celtic Pilot*. Of a mild and sincere nature, I found much in common with him. Deeply interested in radio, he appeared to have a good knowledge of valve theory and could discuss the valve lineup and function of a five-valve superhet with fluent ease. He disliked correspondence of any sort and tended to keep a low profile. On one occasion, the pair of us had been invited to a cocktail party at the Cable & Wireless radio station on St Helena. When we arrived, we stationed ourselves at the opposite side of the room from the island's governor who was also attending and every time he appeared to be edging closer to us, we edged further away. We kept this up all evening and finally crept away and returned to the ship under the cover of darkness.

One day, he appeared in the radio office looking harassed and clutching a sheaf of papers. He had a lot of typing to do and we all knew he didn't like typing. Jeannie, our assistant purser was busy on something else, would I mind doing it? I was in the middle of my radio accounts which was quite a big job and not one of which I was particularly fond. Seeing his downcast countenance, I took the papers off him and promised to type them up as soon as possible. Seeing my accounts, he asked if it would help if he did them for me. This seemed to be a fair exchange, so I folded the lot up and handed them over. An hour or so later, just as I was completing his typing, he returned with the accounts and a great smile on his face. They were done beautifully in his neat handwriting and all balanced perfectly. We then went off for a quiet drink.

In due course, the company was involved in the refit of a large cargo ship called the *Kitmeer*. When this came up, I advised my old friend Dave Webster, former electrical officer of the *Bandama*. He applied to Curnow Shipping and was accepted immediately. On completion of the *Kitmeer*, a permanent vacancy was available on the *St Helena* and he was able to remain in the company.

Over the next few years, the sea staff changed slightly from time to time and a number of former old shipmates joined the company. Others came from a number of big shipping lines that were 'downsizing' their sea staff.

In due course, the company added another small ship to the fleet. This was the 500-ton coastal tanker *Cherrybobs*, which had begun life in 1961 as the *Esso Dover*. After a refit in the UK she was renamed *Bosun Bird* and despatched to St Helena under the initial command of Bob Wyatt. On arrival she became a bunkering vessel and most of her time was spent at anchor in St Helena. When the *St Helena* arrived, we would go alongside the *Bosun Bird* and take on fuel oil. The vessel also supplied many of the small yachts which called at the island with fuel. When she was empty, she would fill up again either on the coast of West Africa, or Walvis Bay in South West Africa. Dry docks were completed in Cape Town. Mainly under the command of Paddy Dodkins, she was probably the smallest tanker engaged on long ocean voyages.

After I had been with Curnow for about a year, I approached them with a view to becoming a shareholder. To my delight, they said that they were looking into the possibility of offering shares to senior officers. In due course they did so, but neither radio officer was included in the offer. The shares were taken up by a number of our shipmates. For quite a while, the rest of us grew weary of the often repeated phrase 'Speaking as a shareholder...' followed by some lofty statement or other. My disappointment was very great, but an alternative major investment which I made against all advice, repaid me sixfold in the fullness of time. So it was eventually a case of "All's well that ends well!" Within a year or two, all the imagined status of being a 'shareholder' had dispersed and been forgotten. In the early 1980s, chief engineer Bryan Gillott did me the honour of asking me to be best man at his wedding in St Helena. I had sailed with Bryan for some time when he was senior 2nd engineer in the liner *Pendennis Castle* and I was 2nd radio officer. The wedding was a lavish affair and well attended by the ship's officers, crew and passengers and many islanders. Everything went smoothly, but it was a hectic day for me and I found it quite unnerving to make a speech before so many people. The register was signed in the Castle at Jamestown with all the ceremony of the vanished British Empire. It was an early rise for all of us as we sailed for Cape Town early the following morning.

I always enjoyed the calls at the islands in the early years. Once the anchor was down and the passengers disembarked, it became very peaceful. Often at Ascension, a group of off-duty officers would go ashore for a picnic to Comfortless Cove which lay round the coast. In the 1840s it was used as a quarantine area for men who had contracted yellow jack, smallpox or any other horrible disease while serving on the island or in the navy. They were apparently landed in the cove with a supply of food and water and simply left either to die or recover! Behind the cove is a small graveyard with stones or rough wooden crosses bearing the names of those who died. Once a grim place which no one wanted to visit, it had become a picturesque spot for a day out! The company also had a small bus on Ascension Island. The purser would take passengers and the occasional officer on day tours of the Island which was mostly a blistering hot scene of volcanic desolation. The top of the island, however, was cool and green owing to the altitude. Right on the very peak sat Green Mountain Farm, an area rich in vegetation and heavily cultivated. A pleasant contrast to the alien landscape below.

St Helena was totally different. Situated further south, the climate was more like a permanent English summer. Externally, the island was of grim and forbidding appearance, but the interior was beautifully green and not unlike the remoter parts of Britain. Visits to Longwood House, where the Emperor Napoleon had

A grave at Comfortless Cove, Ascension Island

21

been confined for his final years were always popular, as were visits to Plantation House, the residence of the governor of the island. In the grounds of Plantation lived Jonathan, the giant tortoise reputedly brought to the island in 1882 and his two smaller female companions, young girls of 80 years or so. Some say Jonathan's age is about 200 years, but whether this is true or not, I cannot say. In the eighteen years that I frequented the island, none of the three have visibly changed and they can still cover the ground at a fair speed if so inclined!

If there were problems with the radio or radar equipment while we were at anchor, I could take the defective units out onto the bridge table and work on them at my leisure. With the circuit diagrams and manuals spread out in the sunshine, occasionally stopping to watch the activity of cargo going on outside, I again congratulated myself on landing such a fine job.

One afternoon at Ascension, the chief officer, Josh Garner, asked me if I would like to assist him in measuring the double bottom tanks of the ship. The company had requested measurements some days earlier. As we lay at anchor overnight, the lids had been removed from the tanks to ventilate them. We descended into the gloomy cavity with the bilge water sloshing chest deep around us. Beneath our feet we did not feel steel plating, but a sand-like substance which lay in a thick deposit. The steel plates and frames around us glistened black and leprous in the light of our torches. It was an eerie sensation to see parts of the ship that never saw the light of day. It was all far removed from the clean comfort of the upper decks and accommodation. On completion of the measurements, we arrived on the bridge wing covered from head to foot in a slimy black substance. Dave Roberts, 2nd officer, immaculate in white uniform, then proceeded to hose us down with salt water until we were sufficiently clean to enter the accommodation again. I always enjoyed such diversions as this as it made a change from communications and electronics. About a year after I joined, the company took on a number of St Helenan apprentices in both the deck and engine room departments. The aim was eventually to man the ship with St Helenan officers as well as crew. The scheme worked out quite well: of the original batch, three gained their chief engineer's certificates and one his master's (captain) certificate. Two of them are still with the *St Helena* at the time of writing. Rodney Young, who has the distinction of being the first Saint to obtain a master's certificate, has risen to the rank of captain of the present ship while David Yon holds the position of chief engineer. During the past twenty years, more apprentices have been taken on, most of them gaining their certificates of competence, whilst some have moved on to other companies, others have remained in the *St Helena*. Over the years, a number of naval officers between the ranks of midshipman and lieutenant

Author and chief officer Josh Garner with 2nd officer Dave Roberts after working in double bottom tanks

commander have also completed voyages in the *St Helena* in order to familiarise themselves with the working of a merchant ship.

As the years passed, we continued our idyllic existence trundling up and down the Atlantic with seldom a care in the world. Everything was running smoothly and our 'Indian Summer' and golden years seemed to have no end. But fate has a habit of intervening when things appear perfect and fate dealt us, and many others, a severe blow as we set out from Avonmouth on 22nd April 1982 at the start of Voyage 25. The Falklands War began.

Chapter 2

Falkland Islands Task Force

On the 20th April, 1982, I rejoined the *St Helena* as normal at Avonmouth. About two weeks previously, a small item had appeared in the national press saying that Argentinian scrap metal dealers had landed on the remote island of South Georgia in order to demolish a disused whaling station. They landed without permission and hoisted the Argentinian flag! Although we were all aware of this, it seemed a minor incident at the time and we went about our business blissfully unaware of the effect it would have on our lives over the next fifteen months.

Our berth at Avonmouth was next to a large swing bridge that could be opened to let ships pass into the inner basin. When I rejoined, I noticed that this bridge was open. It appeared that it had become faulty and because of the complexity of the problem, it would take about eighteen months to repair! This represented a major inconvenience for all of us. In order to leave the dock, we would now have to walk round the edge of the inner basin in order get to the dock gate. This added a considerable distance and what had been a short walk turned into a considerable one. The bridge, in fact, was affecting our lives far more than the incident in far away South Georgia.

We sailed as normal and proceeded on our voyage. As we progressed down the South Atlantic, the situation in the Falklands took on serious proportions when they were invaded by Argentina in early April. A British Task Force was quickly assembled and sent south. When we arrived at Ascension Island, the main Task Force was already there and the usually quiet atmosphere was alive with the bustling activity of numerous warships and merchant vessels. Anchored in the midst of them, working cargo, we could hardly go unnoticed. A senior officer from HMS *Invincible* came across and inspected the ship, planting the thought in our minds that we could well be 'requisitioned'. As the voyage continued, our fears grew. When the Argentinian cruiser *General Belgrano* was torpedoed and sunk on May 2nd, we realised that the situation had gone beyond the point of no return. Two days later, I was awakened at midnight by the 2nd officer with the alarming news that HMS *Sheffield* had been struck by an exocet and, with twenty dead and twenty-four injured, was damaged beyond repair. I spent a sleepless night worrying. With twenty-one years of sea service behind me, I had come to accept that the job had its dangers, but accepted it all as part of the deal. This was different, however: British seamen had been killed and a British warship had been damaged beyond repair by enemy action and not the indifference of the sea.

From then on, the news was all bad. Aircraft of both sides were shot down and a total exclusion zone was set up around the Falklands. An Argentinian supply ship was sunk by HMS *Alacrity* on May 10th. Later the same day, the severely damaged *Sheffield* also sank. By May 12th, the Cunard liner *Queen Elizabeth 2* sailed from Southampton for the Falklands with 3,000 troops aboard. The news was indeed alarming.

On our northern call at Tenerife, a number of senior naval officers again boarded the *St Helena*, to assess whether she was suitable for use as a support ship. They went over the ship from stem to stern and appeared satisfied with what they saw. Shortly after we left Tenerife, it was confirmed officially that we would be requisitioned on arrival at Avonmouth. My workload immediately multiplied to almost impossible proportions. Gigantic stores lists for all departments had to be prepared and sent off as well as the escalating private messages from passengers and crew. For the last few days I was working from about 0800 until well beyond midnight to deal with the communications traffic. In the Bay of Biscay, all hands set to work dismantling the awning spars from the boat deck. Younger passengers also set to with a will, eager to play their part in the unfolding drama.

We were told that only volunteers from the officers and crew would sail south with the ship, no-one would be forced to go if they did not wish it. As we had all been working a voyage on, voyage off system for some time, it was assumed that those on board would simply go on leave as normal and volunteers from the sea staff currently on leave would sail south with the ship. Despite a very real element of apprehension and suppressed fear, most of the officers on board volunteered to go. Although I had no desire to get involved in a war of any kind, I immediately made a firm decision to go if it was at all possible. I had enjoyed working aboard the *St Helena* more than anything that had gone before. The *St Helena* was my life and if the ship went south, I would go as well. I would take the rough with the smooth!

The crew were in a more difficult situation. They lived in St Helena, and if they didn't sail with the ship, how would they get home? We arrived at Avonmouth on 22nd May, 1982. The sailing officers and crew were quickly selected and, much to my relief, I was among them. Initially, it was intended that Neil Abbott would relieve me as normal, but as he was a New Zealander, this was not permitted.

It came as something of a surprise to find that the swing bridge at Avonmouth, which was supposed to be out of service for eighteen months, had been repaired. A number of ships were in dock preparing to sail south and the bridge was essential for cargo work! Our initial orders were to sail that evening for refit in Portsmouth Dockyard. Most of the officers were relieved for this short voyage round the coast, but in my case it was not possible. When we arrived in Portsmouth, Neil arrived for the refit and I was able to go home for a few days.

The week of modification was extensive and hectic. A flight deck and hangar for a Wasp helicopter was fitted over the boat deck. The fresh water tanks were converted into fuel tanks and a reverse osmosis fresh water plant was installed. The osmosis unit produced fresh water from sea water on a daily basis, thus taking the place of our old fresh water tanks. My cabin was converted into a satellite communications centre. Consequently I had to move out. I chose the old 3rd officer's cabin which was at the bottom of the stairs leading up to the radio office and bridge; the 3rd officer moved into a passenger cabin. The existing radio office remained, but although still functional, it was subject to radio silence. Another communications centre was fitted in number four hold inside a large container. An extra radio officer from the Royal Fleet Auxiliary was also appointed to the ship, together with a radio supervisor, leading radio operator and a number of communication ratings. Four 20 mm Oerlikon guns were fitted, two below the lifeboats and another two on the foredeck. The Wasp helicopter was fitted with AS12 missiles. We were to act as a support vessel for two mine hunters, HMS *Brecon* and HMS *Ledbury*, supplying them with everything they needed from fuel to stores. Our jumbo derrick was unshipped from the mast and fitted to the port side of number two mast-house in order to act as a RAS derrick. 'RAS' meant 'Replenishment At Sea'. The derrick swung the oil pipe across to the ship to be refuelled while we were under way. A stern RAS system was also fitted for refuelling in bad weather. In addition to £150,000 worth of stores, we also carried spare main engines for the mine-hunters and extensive workshops in the form of modular Forward Support Units. Extensive spares and test equipment arrived for all departments and I was pleased to find everything that

HMS Brecon

HMS Ledbury *pitching*

I had ordered arrived as if by magic. More mine-sweeping equipment including general stores, ammunition and explosives then came aboard.

During the refit, the news from the South Atlantic was grim. HMS *Ardent* had been sunk the day before we arrived in Avonmouth. On the 23rd, HMS *Antelope* was badly damaged during an air attack and blew up the following day during bomb disposal at San Carlos. The following day, HMS *Coventry* and the big Cunard container ship *Atlantic Conveyor* were both attacked and sunk. I remembered the day, five years previously, when HMS *Coventry* had left the Cammell Laird's shipyard at Birkenhead, immaculate and proud—now she was at the bottom of the sea!

One hot sultry evening in Portsmouth, I went on deck. The air was oppressively hot and the harbour was flat calm. In the setting sun, HMS *Lowestoft* came gliding in without a sound, her flag flying at halfmast. I realised that further bad news had been received and must admit, I felt a rising apprehension concerning the immediate future. I subsequently learned that the RFA ships *Sir Galahad* and *Sir Tristram* has been bombed and severely damaged with the loss of fifty men.

On our last commercial voyage, Lionel Williams, senior engine room rating, was given temporary promotion to 4th engineer. This enabled him to take his wife Brenda along for the voyage. When the ship was requisitioned, both of them volunteered to go south with the ship. In order to accomplish this, Brenda was signed on as a stewardess. Maureen and Glenda, our stewardesses, had also volunteered and despite initial objections by the Navy, they finally relented and let all three go. The officers and crew who did not wish to go with the ship then departed as we sailed for Portland where we were to join up with *Brecon* and *Ledbury* and collect the Wasp helicopter.

The officers who did not sail south with the ship simply went home on leave. The crew, however, were all from St Helena and had to be put up in hotels. During the absence of the *St Helena*, the island still required a ship. Curnow Shipping quickly arranged for the 698-ton *Lady Roslin* to fill the breach. She had been built in 1958 for Imperial Chemical Industries of Glasgow and had been used for the transport of explosives. Quickly refitted to carry twelve passengers, she was renamed *Aragonite*. When she sailed for the island, she was manned by those crew members who had not remained with the *St Helena*.

When the ship was finally ready to sail, the ship's company consisted of a Merchant Navy crew of thirty-three (including officers), and seventy-three Royal Navy personnel (including officers) in the former passenger accommodation. As we no longer carried passengers, the Merchant Navy complement was much reduced. The assistant purser was taken off and assistant catering officer, Stephen Biggs was appointed purser on the *Aragonite*. Neither of our own catering officers sailed with the ship, but one was borrowed from the Blue Star Line for the duration. Dr Bennett, although he had volunteered, was sent on leave and replaced by a naval surgeon. At the last moment, the RFA radio officer was taken off as he was required elsewhere in the Task Force. I was asked if I was happy about this. I was: I had been with the ship for three years and was fully familiar with all my equipment. With RN Petty Officer Paddy Strannix and his number two, Leading Radio Operator George Hindmarch plus all the other RN operators aboard, I felt that we were more than capable of dealing with any communications situation which came up. This proved to be the case and throughout the tour of duty, no friction of any kind disturbed the efficiency of the communications department. The RFA radio officer was a very pleasant man, also from Preston. He took to the *St Helena* immediately and was devastated when taken off for service in another ship.

The Merchant Navy officers who sailed were Captain Smith, Chris Hughes chief officer, Ian Chessum 2nd officer, Steve Quinn 3rd officer, Bob Wilson (author), John McMinn chief engineer, Bob Bendall 2nd engineer, Wally Croston 3rd engineer, Peter Wood 4th engineer, Dave Webster electrical officer. Purser Geoff Shallcross and catering officer Dave Atkinson and chef Joe Laight. In addition Mr Osborne-Cribb, a chief officer from the RFA was appointed to the ship as far as Ascension Island. His job was to acquaint the MN crew with the RAS procedures.

When the crew were asked to volunteer, the wine waiter, Glen Beard was anxious to go. It was quickly pointed out that there would be no call for wine waiters down south. Not to be discouraged, Glen immediately requested that he be transferred to the deck department as a seaman. This request was granted and he fulfilled his temporary position with energy and efficiency throughout the campaign. Merchant Navy crew members were as follows:

Deck Department: Ronnie Johnson (bosun), Peter Sim (bosun's mate), Peter Mercury, Glen Beard, Pat Francis, Donald Bowers, Pat Williams, Willie George.

Engineering Department: Lionel Williams, Patrick Thomas, Ivan Thomas, Colin Lawrence.

Catering Department: Eric Mittens, Wilf Thomas, Pat Ellick, Fenny Thomas, Freddie Green, Glenda Francis, Maureen Jonas, Brenda Williams.

Royal Navy officers attached to the ship were: Lt Cmdr Hammerton, (Senior Naval Officer), Lt Cmdr. Heelas (Wasp pilot), Lt Ball (first lieutenant), Lt Newlands (Forward Support Unit), Lt Baron (Naval surgeon) and Warrant Officers Willis and Howieson.

In Portland we took on further stores and tested the RAS equipment across the harbour. HM ships *Brecon* and *Ledbury* arrived and the Wasp helicopter flew in and executed a perfect landing on our brand-new flight deck.

A Dedication Service for the ship's company was held on the flight deck on the 12th June 1982. Captain Smith addressed the ship's company with the following words:

'Seeing that in the course of our duty, we are set in the midst of many and great dangers and that we cannot be faithful to the high trust placed in us without the help of Almighty God, let us unite in prayers in seeking His blessing upon this ship and all who sail in her, that she may sail under God's good providence and protection, and that there may never be lacking men well qualified to offer in her their work and skill for His greater glory, and for the protection of our realm and dominions.'

This was followed by the hymn 'Lead us Heavenly Father, lead us.' A naval chaplain then blessed the ship and company. This was followed by the Lord's Prayer and then the Naval Prayer:

'O Eternal Lord God, who alone spreadest out the Heavens, and rulest the raging of the sea; who has compassed the waters with bounds until day and night come to an end; be pleased to receive into the Almighty and most gracious protection the persons of us thy servants, and the fleet in which we serve. Preserve us from the dangers of the sea, and from the violence of the enemy; that we may be a safeguard unto our most gracious Sovereign Lady, Queen Elizabeth and her Dominions; and a security for such as pass on the seas upon their lawful occasions; that the inhabitants of our island may in peace and quietness serve thee our God: and that we may return in safety to enjoy the blessings of the land, with the fruits of our labours, and with thankful remembrance of the mercies to praise and glorify thy Holy Name: through Jesus Christ our Lord, Amen.'

After the final blessing, we were stood down. The solemn dignity of the service could not help but move the hardiest of souls and everyone went quietly about their business for some time, each coming to terms with his or her uncertain future and the task that lay ahead.

On 13th June, 1982, we sailed from Portland under radio silence. Shortly after sailing the fleet tanker RFA *Black Rover* moved silently towards us and the RAS derrick and pipes were swung outboard and connected as the two ships sailed on parallel courses only a few feet apart. Next the stern RAS was tested with HMS *Brecon*. On completion of the exercise, *St Helena* took the lead in a 'V' formation, while *Brecon*, and *Ledbury* followed astern of us.

31

As evening fell, the three ships set their course for the South Atlantic. About 2100 that evening, the engines of the *St Helena* stopped and a strong smell of diesel fuel began to permeate through the accommodation. This caused a fair amount of superstitious consternation above decks. I head one leading rate saying to his mates 'She doesn't want to go!' An old saying in the Merchant Navy was 'Growl you may, but go you must.' The old ship was merely 'growling', within minutes the rumble of our stout Werkspoor engine was again beating out its familiar rhythm. The smell of diesel quickly cleared and no further problems were experienced.

Prior to leaving port, all our beds had been stripped of sheets and pillow cases and we were each issued with a sleeping bag. These would be used for the foreseeable future in order to reduce laundry. I found that the twenty-eight years or so since I had last used a sleeping bag as a Boy Scout had not made them any more comfortable. By about 0100, I gave it up and, wrapping myself in a blanket, retired to my hard daybed where I slept soundly for the rest of the night. I never used the sleeping bag again!

The following morning found us proceeding silently south. The first of many exercises then commenced with flying stations and the launch of the helicopter on her first flight. Watching the machine take off, I felt rather nervous seeing how close the flashing blades apparently came to my emergency aerial pole which had been erected on the hangar. Although the pole never seemed to concern the pilot, Lt Cmdr Heelas, its position continued to cause me worry through the voyage. Next came zig-zag procedures and an explanation of RAS procedures by Mr Osborne-Cribb. As darkness fell, the blackout was checked by the helicopter.

On the fourth day out, the *St Helena* completed her first RAS when she successfully fuelled both *Brecon* and *Ledbury* while we were under way. The operation passed off smoothly, and again the Merchant Navy staff experienced the hitherto unknown experience of seeing another ship sailing on a parallel course only a few feet away. In calm weather, the RAS operations were quickly accepted as a normal part of sea life on the part of the MN staff. In bad weather, however, the sight was magnificent and not to be missed. As the ship to be fuelled closed in on the *St Helena*, huge waves would crash back and forth between the two vessels sending up great sheets of solid water and spray, often drenching those working on deck. The pipe would be swung across and connected and despite the maelstrom of water between, the two ships would maintain an exact separation. The *St Helena*, being by far the bigger vessel would plough serenely on. The mine hunters, however, would sometime appear to be about to take off. The bows would leap clear of the water until daylight could clearly be seen beneath their keels almost as far aft as the bridge. Then they would plunge forward into the ocean until their deck was level with the roaring seas which

Aerial view of St Helena *with HMS* Brecon *and HMS* Ledbury

flashed past on either side, before leaping skywards once again. There was normally a seaman on the foredeck tending the lines which extended between the ships. Initially, it seemed that he was in great danger of being washed overboard, but the fibreglass hulls seemed to possess such buoyancy that never once did I see solid water sweep their foredecks during RAS. When we entered the tropics, it was a common sight to see schools of dolphin leaping beneath the bows of the mine hunters when they closed on the *St Helena*.

Flying operations took place on a regular basis and often involved transfer of stores or personnel among the three ships. It was also possible for the officers and crew of the *St Helena* to have a flight in the helicopter on certain occasions. What had, in former times, been our quiet period between 1400 and 1600 daily was now sporadically shattered by the rattling explosions of gunnery practice as our four oerlikons poured their 20 mm shells into either floating targets or target flares. Never in my twenty-one years at sea had I ever imagined that I would see empty shell cases rattling and rolling down the deck of a merchant ship!

On the domestic side, the ship was divided into three. The main lounge was split by a curtain which screened off one third of it. This third, which contained the bar, became the wardroom and was for the use of both RN and MN officers. The remaining two thirds was the petty officers recreation room, while the stern gallery was solely for the use of the ratings. The dining saloon was also divided, the RN and MN officers using what had been the captain's table plus one passenger table when we were on our normal trade. Silver service was dispensed with and our meals were served on the plate by Glenda and Maureen. The petty officers and ratings also ate in the saloon, but in curtained off sections. The standard of the food was maintained at its usual high standard by Joe Laight and the naval cook who worked together in the galley.

Entertainments virtually ceased. A number of tea chests full of paperback books had arrived on board prior to sailing. These were gifts from ordinary people throughout the UK and were much appreciated by all on board. We also had a number of movie films and occasional bingo evenings and that was it. This did not bother us unduly, indeed, it was a pleasure to be able to relax from the continual requirements of entertaining passengers.

The Argentinian surrender had taken place the day after we left Portland, but this did not affect us as we were not going down to fight; our main purpose was mine clearance and a lot of them were still there! Although the islands had been recaptured, the situation still remained unclear. In view of this, the Task Force erred on the side of caution and carried on in a full state of readiness for anything.

Passing through the tropics, it was decided to test the stern RAS facility, but this was not completely successful, for a very unlikely reason. Almost as soon as the lines were run out astern, they were attacked by a number of vicious and hungry sharks. I doubt whether this would have had much effect on the heavy fuel line, but they certainly made their presence felt on the freshwater line. Although I was not present, I was told that as the pipe was hauled aboard, a string of sharks had been lifted from the water. When they reached the level of the poop deck, a rating beat them with a stick until they fell off! Normally, I would not have believed this, but on going aft and inspecting the pipe, I could see it had been completely ruined by numerous teeth marks along its length

As we approached the equator, the Crossing the Line ceremony was eagerly anticipated by members of the RN who had crossed it before. Our own circular swimming pool had been landed before we left the UK in order to make space for extra equipment on deck. A temporary canvas-lined pool was quickly built on number one hatch. The MN staff were not particularly bothered by all the fuss as most of us had crossed the line literally hundreds of times. On the day in question, the reason for their anticipation became more obvious. It seemed to be a tradition that all off-duty RN personnel attended. The MN also went along to join in the 'fun'. It was not the sedate ceremony that we had staged so many times in the past. The junior ratings were dealt with first, and then the petty officers. The treatment was rough, and unpleasant for them. RN and MN 'Old hands' watched the proceedings with glee, cheering on the King and Queen and their muscular officials. Finally came the cream on the cake. The RN officers were brought forth and in the name of 'fun' the court went to work on them. Quickly forced to kneel in order to be 'sentenced,' they were dragged one by one to the chair and given the 'treatment.' At the end of this, their mouths were forced open and a foul potion poured in: then, coughing and spluttering, they were pitched into the pool. None of them seemed to be exempt, although I suspect that more than one of them had Crossed the Line before. The Senior Naval Officer alone escaped this treatment. It was not because of his rank, however— he had gone along with the rest and had wisely 'dressed down' for the occasion. Wearing a drab pullover and collar pulled up round the neck, he also wore a steel helmet which added to the disguise. The ceremony was brought to an abrupt end by the back end of the pool collapsing sending a torrent of water pouring aft down the main-deck. The ceremony was very enjoyable and everyone took it in good part although one of the RN officers told me afterwards that the foul brew forced down him had come very close to making him sick! I wonder how things would have gone if the pool had not collapsed. In any event the RN did not lay a finger on any MN staff officer or crew.

On 26th June, the ship sighted Ascension Island. In Portsmouth, I had purchased an enlarger and a large quantity of printing paper and chemicals so that I could develop and print my own black and white photographs as we went along. I also had three 35 mm cameras and an 8 mm cine camera. It was decided that I should go up in the helicopter and photograph the three ships from the air. This was my first flight and, after being given a safety brief, was fitted into my flying gear by a petty officer of the flight. Throughout the campaign I was very impressed by the general efficiency of the flight deck personnel. Seated in the back of the machine, I looked with some apprehension at the emergency aerial pole on the end of the hangar. Permission was requested of the bridge for take-off and on receiving it we lifted off, dropping astern almost immediately and veering away to one side, looking very much like a mechanical wasp. The doors had been removed, so the sides were open to the floor, but I could not fall out, because I was held in by a safety strap which left me ample space to move. As soon as we took off, *Brecon* closed in to port of the *St Helena* and the RAS connections were set up. Then *Brecon* came in to starboard and began transferring stores and equipment by a light jackstay. During the time we were aloft, I took a complete roll of film including the photograph reproduced in this book. Eventually, when copies of it filtered back to the UK I was to see it in the national press as well as a number of other publications. It was not credited to me, but 'Windjammer', a nickname that I had picked up years ago in the Union-Castle Line because of my keen interest in sailing ships, and although I had not expressly given permission for anyone to use the picture, I was not unduly bothered about it—it was simply an honour to see my photograph enjoying such a high profile! It came as a great surprise to me to find that our altitude had no effect on me. At one stage, I was sitting on the deck, feet dangling over several hundred feet of nothing, clicking away with my camera. I was completely enthralled by the experience of seeing my ship underway so far below. From time to time, the ridiculous thought crossed my mind of what would happen if one of my boots fell off and went down the funnel of a mine hunter, I suppose this was some strange form of subconscious nervousness. When we touched gently down on the flight deck, I was sorry that the time had passed so quickly.

All the time we were proceeding down through the tropics, the reverse osmosis equipment performed so well that we could not consume all the fresh water produced. Two permanent streams of it ran down either side of our foredeck, a very unusual situation in a merchant vessel.

As far as the work was concerned, I was having rather an easy time. Under radio silence, I had no messages to send or receive and spent hours in the radio office sorting and indexing all the spares that had been supplied in Portsmouth and Portland. Because there were no messages to send, I had no accounts to do either and the numerous exercises helped to make life more interesting. The ship did communicate with the UK on a daily basis, but this was all done by the RN operators using encrypted satellite communications. We could receive standard BBC news broadcasts on the overseas service, but I for one was appreciative of our new isolation.

On arrival at Ascension, we had a brief respite before proceeding on our way. A lot of the ship's company took the opportunity to do a bit of shark fishing, while others were able to get ashore and have a look around Georgetown. The Ascension anchorage had altered considerably from the dreamy, peaceful days of only a few months before. There were a number of ships lying at anchor either on their way out or on their way back from the Falklands. Small, high-speed rubber boats were tearing back and forth between ships and the shore. The large bunkering tanker, *Maersk Ascension* had gone and replaced by the *Alvega*, bringing back memories of her launch at Cammell Laird's shipyard, five years previously.

By early evening, all our stores and bunkering had been completed and we sailed for Port Stanley. As we proceeded south in our 'V' formation with *Brecon* in the lead, we came across a Russian cargo ship sailing in the opposite direction. Immediately the three of us had passed, the Russian altered course and joined the formation, sailing abeam of the *St Helena*. This peculiar state of affairs continued for some hours and I was unaware of any communication with the other vessel. By early evening it was still there and our helicopter was launched in order to have a closer look. The Russian ship then turned round and resumed her original course and was soon out of sight. The incident was closed!

As we approached the Falklands, the weather deteriorated and it became bitterly cold. A total exclusion zone of 400 miles had been set up around the islands by the British forces. When we entered this zone, we went into defence stations in full readiness for any attack from Argentina. This involved the ship's company being split into two watches, each watch completing six hours on duty followed by six off. Dress of the day, on or off duty, was flame-proof overalls worn over cotton clothing, anti-flash hoods and gloves, folded lifejackets worn on the belt ready for inflation, identity tags, and field dressing packs worn on the belt. Geneva Convention identity cards were also to be carried at all times. In addition to this, we all had to carry a bulky survival suit and gas mask. I was attached to the bridge staff as the RN were dealing with all communications. At night, we were allowed to take off our boots and lifejackets, but had to have them immediately to hand. The nights in the Total Exclusion Zone were long and uncomfortable. All exposed personnel, lookouts, gun crews and bridge staff were issued with steel helmets and the captain and senior naval officer, flack jackets. The order was also given for all beards to be shaved off—this was to facilitate a perfect fit for the gas masks.

During defence watches, twenty minutes were allowed for meals which were still taken in the dining saloon. Crockery was not used, but the food was doled out on to tin trays with indentations in them. The food continued to be of high quality with rainbow trout being served on one occasion. (I was less than impressed with this, however, not being a fish lover!)

On the 9th July, 1982, as we wearily approached the islands, a faint glimmer of light was reported by one of the lookouts. Our radar sets were not in use as they could be detected by the enemy at great distance if switched on. It was decided to turn the main radar on for a single sweep which would only give about one second of transmission. As the sweep went round, we saw that we were absolutely surrounded by a vast number of ships. This, we hoped, was the main British Battle Group. Almost immediately, a faint red light began winking Morse code at us. As we stood on the freezing bridge wing, everyone who knew Morse (except me), began calling out the individual letters as they were sent. Although they called out the letters correctly, the end result was that when it was completed, the message had not actually been received. All that had happened was that a jumble of individual letters had been chanted to no one in particular! The RN signalmen would have had no problem, but they were all busy in their various communication modules. All eyes were turned on me. 'What did it say?' someone asked. 'I have no idea!' I replied, 'I couldn't think straight for all the letters being called out. When they send it again, please keep quiet!' As we did not acknowledge, the message was repeated. Each time the light flickered, I mentally converted it to a sound in my head. In this way, the only difference to receiving Morse by wireless, was that lamp Morse is a lot slower. The message was quickly received and when it was complete, I repeated it to the onlookers. Once it was established that we were under the protection of the main Task Force, our growing fears were allayed.

The following morning we sighted the Falklands. It was a freezing cold day with a watery sun peering through the mist and snow. Our decks were lightly dusted with a covering of ice and frozen snow and most of us were feeling very tired. It came as a relief to find that a smaller naval ship was to escort us into the harbour of Port Stanley. As we sailed through the entrance most eyes were turned towards the town, but mine were rivetted on the canted hulk of the iron barque *Lady Elizabeth* which lay beached in Whalebone Cove at the eastern end of the big harbour. The old sailing ship had been built as far back at 1879 in Sunderland and had been hulked at Port Stanley in 1913 after suffering severe damage off Cape Horn. For many years I had wanted to visit the Falklands in order to see the many sailing ship wrecks which littered the islands. Although I would have wished the visit to have been under more peaceful circumstances, I was nevertheless pleased to have arrived at last.

We anchored in the middle of the harbour and *Brecon* and *Ledbury* came and tucked themselves up alongside us and we settled down for the night. Shortly after our arrival, we were stood down from defence watches and were able to dress more comfortably. As darkness fell, we received warnings of an impending air raid and the guns were duly uncovered and lookouts posted. We saw the flames from the jet exhausts on the airfield as the Sea Harriers took off to intercept any approaching enemy. In due course the aircraft all returned and the raid did not materialise. For the next year or more this was to be repeated on a regular basis every two or three nights. Fortunately, no enemy aircraft got through and we never saw any enemy action whatsoever!

During the night it snowed heavily and on waking, the entire shoreline was deep in snow. The sky was cloudless and a brilliant sun shone over Port Stanley and the ships in harbour. There were warships, mine sweepers, Royal Fleet Auxiliary ships, converted passenger liners, hospital ships, ferries and cargo ships. More ships, including the big oil tankers lay outside in Port William Sound. Coming and going between the ships were small high speed boats, tugs and all manner of small craft. The air was alive with helicopters from tiny Wasps to the gigantic Chinooks with their double rotors and spacious bodies.

Scanning the harbour with my binoculars, I was quickly able to find most of the sailing ship wrecks. *Lady Elizabeth* was the most prominent followed by the big American packet ship *Charles Cooper* which had arrived in 1866. Then there was the East Indiaman *Jhelum* which had been built at Liverpool in 1849 and arrived in Port Stanley in 1870. Only a few broken frames remained of the little

Welsh barque *Capricorn*, but this was not surprising as she had been built in 1829. Only the stern was visible of the big 1,006-ton Canadian barque *Egeria* which had been built in 1858 in Quebec. There were more wrecks, not immediately visible, but more of these later.

Shortly after arriving in Port Stanley, *Brecon* and *Ledbury* went about their mine-hunting duties off the entrance, leaving us on our own. We required a small amount of petrol, and were advised that this could be obtained from one of the tankers in Port William Sound. A lifeboat was lowered in charge of Steve Quinn, 3rd officer and with Dave Webster electrical officer, Peter Wood 4th engineer and myself aboard, together with seamen Donald Bowers, Pat Francis and Pat Williams, we set off for the tanker. The time was about 1000 and the weather was fine, cold and sunny. In due course, we arrived alongside and passed our empty cans up and settled down to wait. The wait was long and cold, but finally the filled cans were slung down to us and we cast off. Heading back towards Port Stanley, the weather seemed to get colder and darker. Then, to add to our problems, the engine spluttered and died. Peter diagnosed a fuel blockage and began trying to clear it with numbed fingers. This proved impossible and we began to drift slowly seawards. We had a handheld VHF walkie-talkie aboard, but all efforts to summon help fell on deaf ears. We drifted slowly past the big hospital ship *Uganda* lying at anchor in the sound, her huge white hull with its red crosses almost blending into the snow-covered shoreline beyond. No one seemed to take any notice of us and we began to feel like lumps of ice. Eventually, a small battered army landing craft, minus its front door, wallowed towards us and asked if we needed assistance. A line was thrown across and they proceeded to tow us alongside a tanker also lying at anchor. We tied up alongside after the army lads explained that they had other business to attend to, but promised to return for us on completion. Slowly and painfully, we boarded the ship and found our way to the bridge. The captain was most sympathetic and detailed someone to take us down to the crews' recreation room which was warm and smoke filled. She was a British-crewed ship and the seamen made us welcome, supplying us with various drinks and exchanging yarns of our experiences. We remained there for some time, but no sooner had we begun to feel warm again, but the landing craft came back for us. The swell was getting up by then and on going down the pilot ladder, we had to wait until the small craft rose to the level of our feet and then quickly step across, where the soldiers assisted us down. There was no margin for error or hesitation. The penalty for getting it wrong could be any one of three alternatives: either get crushed between the boat and the ship, fall into the sea between them or fall into the landing craft itself. Fortunately, we all made it without mishap. It sounds worse in the telling, at the time I don't think any of us thought much about it, we were just pleased to be going back to the ship. As the long tow back began, the darkness became complete and snow began to swirl around. Steve and Peter remained in the lifeboat to steer it, while the rest of us went below into the scant comfort of the bare steel cabin. The soldiers, it appeared, actually lived aboard, so we were able to see at first hand the hardships they had to endure even when they were not actually fighting!

When we finally came alongside the *St Helena* and climbed back into the warmth and light, we were greeted by our bosun, Ronnie Johnston, who declared with a grin that we looked dreadful, although his exact wording was rather different. It was 1900 hours, and we had been out since mid morning!

During the next few days it was decided that while the ship was at anchor, the three Merchant Navy deck officers who normally kept watches of eight hours duration, followed by eight hours off, would be assisted by two more officers. The watches would then be four hours on duty, followed by sixteen off. The two extra watch-keepers were designated as Warrant Officer Howieson, RN, and yours truly, Wilson MN! Because of the large number of RN communications staff aboard, it appeared that I was largely redundant and the most sensible thing to do was to give me a watch to keep. After twenty-one years as a radio officer, this did not sit lightly on my shoulders. I had no objection as such to taking the job on and was more than willing to 'do my bit'. Whether I was up to it or not was a different matter. The keeping of bridge watches was not in itself a difficult task provided one had the aura of command. As officer of the watch, I had to co-ordinate practically everything that went on until such a time as I was relieved by someone else.

In a merchant ship, public address broadcasts could be made from the purser's office, or bureau as it was known. In naval ships, broadcasts were referred to as 'pipes' and could only be made from the bridge by the officer of the watch. In fact everything had to be channelled through the bridge. With a helicopter on board, this also included 'flying stations'. This small Wasp was an essential part of the mine-hunting team conducted by *Brecon* and *Ledbury*. It set up navigational equipment on various parts of the islands in order to guide and assist the two mine-hunters. Green and red lights were set up on the flight deck and when the pilot and his crewman were aboard, they would call the bridge for permission to start the Wasp's engine. The officer of the watch then gave permission and the rotors would start to spin. They would then request permission to take off and the officer of the watch would switch the lights from red to green. The Wasp would then take off and report to the bridge when airborne. I was quick to point out at the outset that I knew nothing of helicopters and flying or whether wind conditions etc. were safe for take-off or landing. The pilot assured me that it was just a formality that had to be gone through and if it were not safe to take-off or land, he would not do so regardless of what I said! This made me feel a lot easier, but I always breathed a sigh of relief when I saw the machine was safely airborne and wheeling away from the ship. Likewise, I was invariably relieved when the landings were successfully completed and the sound of the rotors died away.

The main duty was keeping a sharp lookout and ensuring that the ship was not dragging her anchor in the gales which could spring up without warning. Every half hour or so, I took visual bearings on a number of easily identifiable points round the harbour. For me, the best points were the wrecks: I could take visuals of the mainmast of *Lady Elizabeth*, the sterns of *Charles Cooper* and *Jhelum*, while on the other side was the badly damaged RFA *Sir Tristram*, a grim reminder of a war which may not yet be over.

As all 'pipes' had to go through the bridge, they took up a goodly proportion of the daylight hours. No longer did I 'request' someone to call at the radio office at their convenience, but issued a command such as a curt '1st lieutenant—bridge!' or whoever else was required. The only concession to this was reserved for the captain who was 'requested' to come to the bridge.

Our chief officer, Chris Hughes, was very helpful and gave me a lot of sound advice on watch-keeping. It was best to keep one wheelhouse door open during the hours of darkness, no matter how cold it got. In this way if the wind got up, it could be heard, where it might not be seen in the darkness of the blackout. Keeping a door open in the Falklands winter was no joke, but as soon as our 2nd engineer, Bob Bendall, heard about this he quickly set to work bringing the bridge radiators back to life, which had lain dormant ever since the ship was employed on the Alaska run as the *Northland Prince*.

During the night watches, the officer of the watch always had a naval rating on duty with him to act as an extra lookout, or run any errands. On my first night watch, the rating approached at about 2200 and asked 'Coffee, sir?' 'Yes please,' I replied. Normally, if a Merchant Navy officer wanted a coffee in the night he made it himself. Then came the question 'Sugar and milk, sir?' 'Yes please!' I replied. To my astonishment he also carried it over to where I stood and actually stirred it up for me! There was no conversation other than that which concerned the ship and any that did occur was liberally spliced with 'Yes, sir', 'No sir' or 'Aye aye sir!' A far cry from a few months previously when I had to put up with the occasional 'Hey, Sparky, I wanna phone call!' After so many years in a more relaxed environment, I always felt uneasy about my new situation, although I appreciated that it was essential for discipline on naval vessel.

If the mine-hunters came alongside, which they could do at any time, requesting spares or equipment, it again had to be done through the bridge. This, however, did not involve much action on the part of the officers of the watch. If the hatches needed opening, I only needed to telephone the buffer and the bosun. (The buffer was the Royal Navy equivalent of our bosun.) They would rouse the required men, while I telephoned the engine room for power on the winches and also to turn on any necessary deck lights. During my previous life as a radio officer, if anything went wrong, it was always up to me to fix it. I never quite got over the feelings of guilt when I issued orders from the comfort of the bridge and they were carried out 'at the double' often in freezing and unpleasant conditions.

Despite any orders being carried out immediately, I always felt easier when either Ronnie Johnson, bosun, or former wine waiter Glen Beard were around. Ronnie was of moderate height, but heavily built and extremely strong. Glen, on the other hand, was extremely tall and fierce looking and, it was rumoured, possessed awesome fighting qualities, although I was never to see him in action. He always seemed to bellow at the top of his voice no matter what the occasion, his statements generally ending in 'Sah!' delivered sergeant major style. Our other seamen, bosun's mate Peter Sim, together with seamen Donald Bowers, Peter Mercury and Pat Francis were equally co-operative and efficient, but of much gentler natures!

Although I had often thought in the past that it would be agreeable to be a ship's captain or a purser and have no technical responsibilities whatsoever, I began to realise that it may not necessarily be a good thing. It is all very well to issue commands or defect notes for others to carry out but issuing a command to fix a broken lawnmower would not have much effect in retirement.I recalled that a dozen years or so previously, I was in the radio office of a large passenger liner when the captain entered clutching a can of gas and a cigarette lighter. 'Can you fill this for me please, Mr Wilson?' he asked, 'It's my first gas lighter!' The words of an ancient piece of sea doggerel came to my mind:

Twice twenty thousand tons of steel obey his sole command,
He rules, a king, whose slightest word is law from land to land!

And yet—he couldn't fill his lighter!

Initially, shore parties were to be in organised groups. The first one, which was Merchant Navy consisted only of half the crew and three officers. Of the three officers, I was appointed to take charge, keep the group together and make sure nobody did anything untoward. It was a bright sunny day when we landed on a jetty built over the wreck of the barque *Margaret*. As soon as we were all ashore, the two other officers in the party promptly headed towards the town, paying not the slightest heed to the order to stay in a group. Apart from being annoying, I felt this also undermined my authority with the crew, although my concern proved to be without foundation. When we arrived back, I brought up the subject of the two errant officers, and to my utter amazement it was dismissed as being OK! However, any ideas of further 'organised parties' were dropped immediately: from then on, we all 'did our own thing' when ashore.

Within days of arriving at Port Stanley, our reverse osmosis plant failed, so fresh water had to be rationed. The failure was not exactly a technical one: the seawater intakes had become choked up with krill. Krill, a small shrimp-like marine crustacean found in great quantity around the Falklands, is the principal food of whalebone whales. The water rationing brought about further problems. As far as living was concerned, we could put up with it—such things were to be expected in the circumstances. The ship, however, was by then nineteen years old and well past the first flush of youth. With the water turned off for several hours a day there was no pressure in the pipes, and the hot water pipes went cold. When it was turned back on, the pressure suddenly reappeared together with a vast flow of hot water as everyone took advantage of it. The constant expansion and contraction began to take its toll on the ageing plumbing and leaks began to appear. Some of these were merely drips, but the more serious ones ranged from a steady flow to a downpour. The port and starboard alleyways at times looked like a film set for a damaged submarine with water pouring in at various rates along the length. Buckets and bins were placed beneath the less serious leaks, while the harassed engine-room staff dealt with the more serious ones. It rapidly became obvious that more than 90% of the bursts occurred in the passenger accommodation now occupied by the naval officers and ratings. As it is commonly thought that ships are possessed of both soul and character, the superstitious wondered whether the old ship was declaring her displeasure at being put to a use for which she was not intended. The krill resulted in the reverse osmosis plant continuing its erratic behaviour throughout our time around the Falklands Islands.

On the 15th July, the mine-hunters had completed their immediate tasks and we proceeded out of the harbour to the tanker *Fort Toronto* which was filled with fresh water rather than oil. With our water tanks full, we fuelled from another tanker, the *G. A. Walker*. On completion of bunkering, we set sail for San Carlos arriving the following day. We anchored three cables from Ajax Bay jetty, opposite the abandoned refrigeration plant that had been converted into a British field hospital where the medical teams had operated on the wounded in the most appalling conditions only a few weeks before. One hundred and seven major operations were conducted in this makeshift hospital which was strafed and bombed a number of times during the battle. Every wounded British soldier brought here alive survived, a tribute to the dedication of the medical staff.

The Scots Guards were still living in the plant when we arrived and I took the opportunity to spend a day with them. Despite the cold, it was reasonably warm inside and the food was quite appetising, although the general living conditions were rather depressing.

The weather, although calm, was dull and cold. When we came to anchor it was in a dense fog. It lifted slightly after a few hours and we could see the ghostly shape of the abandoned Argentinian transport ship *Bahia Buen Sucesso*, lying at anchor a few hundred yards away. This was the ship which began it all when she arrived in Grytviken, South Georgia, to hoist the Argentinian flag. Life in San Carlos, as far as the *St Helena* was concerned, was less hectic than it had been in Port Stanley. *Brecon* and *Ledbury* were away most of the time on mine disposal and wreck location. In addition to the mine clearance, the wrecks of HMS *Coventry* and HMS *Ardent* were located. The remains of HMS *Antelope* lay not too far from where we were anchored and the bay still had a thin sheen of oil.

During a shore visit, we were able to visit the graveyard where a brand new Union Flag flew permanently from the staff. This was a cold, grim and depressing scene still littered with the rubble of war. The crosses were simple wood affairs and it would be some time before the area was transformed into a place of tranquil

The Red Ensign flying over a Rapier missile site

beauty. Considerably later, when I saw the completed cemetery on TV at home, clean and peaceful in the summer sunshine, I simply could not equate the scene with what I had actually witnessed in July 1982.

On seeing a Red Ensign (the flag of the British Merchant Navy) flying on the hillside, several of us headed towards it. We found a rapier missile site guarding the end of their anchorage. The soldiers, finding out that we were Merchant Navy, seemed rather apologetic about the use of the flag, saying it was the only British one they could find, but we were able to assure them that its presence over a British Army installation caused us no upset whatsoever—we were as proud to see it flying on the land as at sea.

During most evenings, a lone piper emerged from the refrigeration plant and began to play. I had always liked pipe music and appreciated the traditional Scottish airs that floated across the depressing scene night after night. Since then, every time I hear bagpipes, my mind is transported to the days when we lay at anchor in San Carlos Water.

One morning, as I came off watch at 0800, Captain Smith advised me that a group of officers had received permission to board the abandoned *Bahia Buen Suceso*. This ship had aroused our curiosity from the start. As well as being the instrument which had indirectly started the war, she had a more than passing resemblance to the *St Helena*. The Lloyds Register told us that she had been built in Canada in 1950, and we wondered if she was designed for the Vancouver–Alaska coastal passenger trade but ended up being sold to Argentina.

The officers going across were Captain Smith himself and all heads of department: chief officer Chris Hughes, chief engineer John McMinn, electrical officer Dave Webster and purser Geoff Shallcross. Being as much a head of department as the electrical officer and the purser, I asked if I could go, but my request was declined as the boarding party was to be kept as small as possible. Being rather tired, I didn't press the point, saying that I would turn in for a few hours, cunningly added that it would have been nice to have a photographic record of the visit. I had hardly settled down when there was a tap on the door and the captain's head appeared: 'Get ready quickly', he said, 'You can come. Don't forget the camera!' Together with a naval officer and a number of ratings, we set off for the derelict. It was a bright day, but very cold. Coming alongside the starboard side, we saw a bedraggled pilot ladder hanging down the side. The ship had obviously come under fire before she was abandoned as there were shell holes in the bridge front. One by one we carefully climbed aboard, each in turn noting that one side of the rope ladder was almost chafed through where it passed over the bulwarks.

The ship was as silent as the tomb and presented a scene of utter dereliction. Rubbish was strewn all over the place and doors had been bursted open. The purser's safe door was hanging open and empty and the whole place smelled dank and dirty. With the aid of torches we looked into some of the cabins and larger rooms: there was no sign of any personal property around, the ship had been thoroughly looted! Some of the rooms had a foot of water in them. The bridge was in a similar condition and even the ship's wheel had been removed. Several portholes had been chiselled off and left on the deck as if the looters had been disturbed. Going into the radio office I found that the equipment racks were all empty with only the connecting wires and plugs hanging from the spaces where the equipment had been. A shell had apparently passed through the small hatch used for communicating between bridge and radio office and exited through the small porthole in the after bulkhead without exploding.

When our inspection was complete, the Merchant Navy staff lined up for a photograph on the boat deck which was covered in a layer of frozen snow. From the resulting picture, one could never have imagined us as we had appeared formerly aboard the passenger liner *St Helena*. We gingerly climbed down the pilot ladder and back into the boat, leaving the derelict ship swinging idly to her anchor. Despite belonging to the enemy, she had presented a melancholy sight and it was not good to see a ship so treated. Eventually, I believe, she was towed out to sea and sunk by gunfire.

By the 26th of July we were back in Port Stanley again. On the 28th, our anchors dragged in the middle of the night and both RN and MN were called at short notice. After a spell of frantic activity, a firm holding ground was again secured. During our time in the Falklands, our anchors dragged on a number of occasions but, to my relief, it never happened when I was on watch.

About the same time, one of our RN ratings, M. E. M. MacDonald was taken ill with appendicitis and sent ashore to the hospital, where he was operated on successfully.

During my time as a bridge watch-keeper my confidence in dealing with the everyday matters of a mine-hunter support ship gradually improved. Inevitably though, I had to learn how to deal with 'mission impossible' orders from outside. On the first occasion I was given an order to accomplish in five to ten minutes, but my estimation was that it would take twenty minutes to half an hour. To add to the problem, it was the middle of the night and all the crew had turned in. Unfortunately, when given the order over the VHF short range radiotelephone, I said that although I would do my best, I felt that there was insufficient time. A snappy and bad-tempered reply came back to the effect that I was to execute the order immediately and never mind 'doing my best!' I did not argue, and telephoned the buffer and the bosun, passing the order on. By the time they and their team reached the bridge it was too late: the moment of crisis had passed, happily without any undue problems.

Next morning, nothing was said to me about the incident or the fact that the order hadn't even been started, let alone completed. The issuing officer seemed to bear me no malice and was his normal polite self when our paths crossed during the day. Eventually, I could bear it no longer and approached another RN about the incident. His advice was that I should have simply said 'Aye, aye, sir!' and passed the order on to the buffer and bosun without comment. Then, if anything was said later, the correct answer would be: 'I passed the order on to the buffer and bosun at 0530 hours, sir!' while at the same time adopting a slightly puzzled look as to why it had not been carried out. He then added that it was very likely that the officer who initiated the order probably realised it was impossible because of the time factor shortly after he issued it, hence the lack of any comments the following day!

Armed with this sound advice, I looked forward to my next 'mission impossible,' so that I could exercise my new-found naval expertise. This came when one of the ships approached to pick up some food stores. The stores list had been received some time before and everything was lying in a cargo net attached to the derrick wire and the bosun was standing by at the cargo winch. As the ship was hovering about fifty feet away and not moving, I asked when it was coming alongside as we were ready. 'No, time!' came the annoyed-sounding reply, 'Put it in our rubber boat!' Their small rubber dinghy, powered by an outboard motor, was just arriving alongside us. The stores on our deck were out of sight of the bridge of the other ship, but it was clear to me that they were actually physically larger than the dinghy. The stock reply of 'Aye, aye, sir,' therefore seemed inappropriate as I did not want to sink the boat. I replied in a similarly forceful tone that the stores were bigger than the boat and would not fit in. On this occasion, my advice was taken—after a short pause, the reply came back 'OK, just send the spuds across!' The potatoes were passed down on their own and shortly afterwards the other ship was wheeling away to her duties again with a wave of acknowledgement from her bridge.

On the 31st July, most of the mine clearance was complete and a cocktail party for the Senior Naval Officer, Falkland Islands, was held aboard the St Helena as we lay in Port Stanley Harbour. By all accounts it was a huge success, but as I was keeping the 2000–midnight watch that evening, I missed it. Three days later a few officers from the St Helena went ashore to the junior school where I put on one of my illustrated slide shows to the children. They had grown up surrounded by derelict sailing ship hulks and it was an eye-opener for many of them to see what they had been like in their prime.

On the 14th August 1982, the three ships sailed for home. In the early evening HMS Brecon, white ensign curling in the breeze, hove in her anchor and set off up the harbour zig-zagging through the anchored ships. She was followed closely by HMS *Ledbury* with the intention of us following on. When it came to our turn, however, we discovered that our anchor cables were twisted and the anchors could not be hove in. One of the big tugs came along and proceeded to push us round in circles to disentangle them. This operation took several hours and we finally left the harbour under cover of darkness. By the following morning we had caught up with our companions and with *Brecon* leading the 'V' formation, we set a course for Ascension Island. I was greatly relieved to be free of my bridge watch-keeping duties, and returned to the radio office content to leave command and organisation to others.

Shortly after clearing the islands, the krill which had plagued our reverse osmosis plant since our arrival, disappeared and the unit began running at full efficiency again. As we passed Buenos Aires, radio silence was lifted for the first time since arrival at Portsmouth almost three months before. It was decided that the RN would deal with all official communications and satellite telephone calls, while I would take on private radio communications for both the RN and MN staff. Naturally, there was a mad rush of private telephone calls home, and I bore the brunt of this. Although the RN could dial straight through with a satellite call, my 'old-fashioned' single-sideband short wave equipment was only a fraction of the cost and therefore proved more popular. Nevertheless, I was not unduly overworked as naval discipline came to my assistance. When we were following our normal trade as a passenger ship with a single radio officer, both passengers and crew would trickle up continually. I normally put calls through whether I was on duty or not. Speaking with the RN communications petty officer, I was advised that private calls were invariably done in blocks at certain hours. So every few days I would start the calls at a certain time and continue until they were all finished which usually took between four and five hours a time, but in the absence of RN or company communications I was not over pressed.

Shortly after leaving Port Stanley, the following message was received from the Senior Naval Officer, Falkland Islands:

> 'I have been impressed by your team's CAN DO attitude and your ability to get on with the job independently and with the minimum of fuss. Well done! Bon voyage and safe homecoming.'

As the ship sailed further north, it was decided to call in at St Helena in order to land any of the crew who wished to go on leave. We all looked forward to this call and the opportunity to get ashore in a sunny port far away from the seemingly eternal ice and cold of the Falklands. On the 25th August, 1982, the RN officers, petty officers and ratings were all dressed in their best, lining the flight deck and bridge top as we approached the anchorage at Jamestown. The MN officers and crew were likewise lining the rails. We had radioed ahead to the governor advising our estimated time of arrival. Passing the anchored *Bosun Bird* we got a few waves from her small crew, but the wharf appeared to be deserted. Eagerly scanning the seafront for some signs of a welcoming committee, we were to be disappointed. A few families and friends of our Saint crew were there and that was all—rather a 'damp squib'! The governor had apparently not considered it necessary to mark the arrival by anything special; in the past we had seen returning football teams treated with more enthu-siasm—such is life!

On anchoring, everyone was stood down and eventually the customs and immigration launch came out to us to complete the formalities. When shore leave was granted, everyone off duty, poured ashore where they were greeted with some enthusiasm by the hospitable islanders. There was widespread annoyance amongst the population that they had been pretty much kept in the dark about our arrival and more than a few apologised profusely, although it was not their fault! Despite the anti-climax of our arrival, everyone was made welcome and a grand time was had by all. The following day, the governor put on a reception and cocktail party for the ship's officers and senior ratings at Plantation House. A fair number of us went along and the rather belated event was hailed as a success.

Next day, the three ships sailed for Ascension Island. Although some of the Saints had left to go on leave, a handful opted to remain in order to see the commission out completely. This placed an added burden on the single RN steward, but he coped admirably with the extra workload.

We refuelled alongside the tanker *Alvega* on arrival at Ascension. As we lay alongside, Dave Webster and I were pleased to recognise a number of former shipmates from our time in Silver Line. Captain Tester, late of the *Bandama* was in command and he invited Dave and I across for lunch, together with Captain Smith, and one or two others. We were all hoisted across on a wooden seat on the end of a derrick wire. It was certainly good to be in hot weather again.

On sailing from Ascension, discipline relaxed and we all settled down for a leisurely voyage home. Crossing the Line certificates were awarded to those who were 'initiated' on the southbound leg of the voyage. Deck buffets and parties were held on the flight deck from time to time, during which everyone intermingled from captain and senior naval officer down to the junior ratings. On one occasion, I inadvertently upset the apple cart at a 'beer party'. When we had left Portsmouth, I decided to stop drinking beer for the duration and limit myself to three glasses of white wine per day. I had successfully kept this up to the extent that I didn't really fancy drinking beer any more, so I took a bottle of wine along. Seated at a small table with the helicopter pilot and one of the petty officers, I commenced to share my bottle of wine. It wasn't long before the first lieutenant came running across complaining that it was a beer party and wine was not allowed! The pilot and petty officer immediately apologised and shoved off. I was in no mood to be denied my wine so I remained seated, with wine glass firmly in hand. The first lieutenant, on seeing that he wasn't getting anywhere, rushed across to Chris Hughes, the MN chief officer, and related the tale to him. Chris was over like a shot, grinning wildly and offering his empty glass in order for it to be filled with wine. The first lieutenant, on finding another recalcitrant officer drinking wine, took his grievance to Captain Smith. Within moments, he had also joined us and when Number One saw three grinning MN officers clutching glasses of wine, he gave up and went away.

Naval operations continued every few days with the necessary refuelling of *Brecon* and *Ledbury* and transferring stores or personnel by helicopter, but gunnery practice and other formerly essential warfare exercises were discontinued.

We were all delighted to hear that we were to put in to Gibraltar for a couple of days' rest. The ship's company was split into two watches so that everyone could take advantage of a run ashore or whatever they wished to do. We arrived on the 7th September and were met by Curnow Shipping's Managing Director Andrew Bell, who was able to bring us up to date with company activities.

The tiny *Aragonite*, although she had proved successful, was far too small for the run as she only carried twelve passengers. They therefore negotiated a charter of the Straits Shipping Company's passenger cargo liner *Centaur*. Straits Shipping was a subsidiary of the famous Blue Funnel Line and the *Centaur* was normally on the Hong Kong–Australia run. She had a passenger capacity of 190 and was also fitted for the transport of 4,500 live sheep as well as general cargo. She was currently en route for Avonmouth from Singapore. A number of Curnow pursers and catering ratings had flown out to join the ship. It was thought that the Ministry of Defence would require the *St Helena* for some time to come and *Centaur* would fill the gap until our return. It was also hinted at that she may well replace the *St Helena* on a permanent basis. This was greeted with much enthusiasm, but we were less pleased to hear that we may have to return to the Falklands again.

We all thoroughly enjoyed our stay in Gibraltar, but were pleased to be finally going home. As we headed north, we received orders to proceed to Rosyth, Scotland, the home port of the mine-hunters. The weather in the Bay of Biscay was excellent with calm seas and bright sunshine every day. On leaving the bay we proceeded to sail past Portland, where our sturdy little helicopter and the flight crew left us. They flew around the ship a few times, posing for photographs and then, with a final wave, buzzed off, very much like a wasp from which the machine took its name.

We passed the White Cliffs of Dover on another beautiful sunny day and again enjoyed a party for all hands on the flight deck. I overheard one of the Royal Navy petty officers saying that the *St Helena* was 'clapped out' and would probably go to scrap when we got back. I took him to task about this saying that the rust and damage was largely superficial and the hazards of the sea were accepted on a daily basis in the Merchant Navy, adding that the ship was certainly fit for a few more years. He disagreed and said if anyone was fool enough to send her south again, she probably wouldn't get there! How wrong he was. A further half million and more miles of ocean was to pass beneath the keel of our stout ship before she was sold for 'further trading'! As we passed through the Dover Straits, the navy began sorting out stores and equipment for landing on arrival at Rosyth.

Shortly before arrival, a final sail past was staged. *St Helena* drew ahead of the formation and at a given signal, the two mine-hunters advanced on us from astern, one on either side. As they drew abeam, we all trained our fire hoses on each other and before they had passed, everyone foolish enough to remain outside, including myself, was thoroughly soaked! After anchoring for the night, we

Aragonite, Centaur *and* St Helena *at Ascension Island*

proceeded slowly up the Firth of Forth and under the Forth Bridge where we docked at the naval base in brilliant sunshine. Family and friends were waiting as the three rather battered looking ships came alongside on the 16th September, 1982. Lunch for the ship's company, family and friends was provided in the form of a cold buffet in our dining saloon.

On the way home we had become accustomed to the battered looking appearance of *Brecon* and *Ledbury*, but seeing the *St Helena* in sunshine from the shore, we were in for another shock. The already battered bulwarks had picked up further dents and twists sustained through the constant comings and goings of the two mine-hunters as well as our having to lay alongside the tankers and general cargo ships during replenishment operations. The normally pristine hull was liberally streaked with rust although not as badly as the decks. Physically, we were probably much fitter than before we started. The high standard of food had been maintained throughout, and we all had plenty of exercise owing to the fact that going or returning from the shore normally meant climbing up and down vertical pilot ladders as well as the need to clamber across other ships that usually lay alongside. Similar activities were also necessary at the many battered jetties of Port Stanley and San Carlos.

Most of the *St Helena*'s officers had been advised that they would be relieved on arrival at Rosyth. Unfortunately, someone in the office had told the reliefs not to hurry back, but arrive 'at their convenience', as it was such a long way! This was not very well received considering that most of us had done not only a normal voyage, but also a further three months in less than ideal conditions. As a result, our families departed without us later that evening, leaving us to cool our heels aboard until the relief column pitched up.

Two days later they arrived and we were free to go. By then it had been decided that the ship was to proceed to Teesport for essential repairs before sailing for the Falkland Islands again, this time as a store ship and troop transport. She was scheduled to operate on a run between Ascension Island, Port Stanley and South Georgia.

It was not until some time after that we discovered the extent of the operations performed by the three ships during the commission. As well as mine clearance, the wrecks of HM ships *Antelope*, *Ardent* and *Coventry* had to be located in order to recover some of their equipment. Five Argentinian fighter aircraft which had not been reported as being shot down were discovered on the seabed. The sunken Argentinian supply ship *Rio Carcarana* was also located in Falkland Sound, her ensign flying in the current. She had been sunk by Sea Harriers from HMS *Hermes* on the 16th May.

Weather conditions had, at times, been atrocious and wind speeds of between 75 and 90 knots had been experienced. The total distance covered was just over

17,000 miles and the ship had refuelled the mine-hunters on twenty-nine occasions. As well as all this, numerous visitors had enjoyed the hospitality of the *St Helena* and the Navy agreed that the three small ships had achieved a minor technological triumph in operating with independent efficiency so far from home.

Despite all this, the South Atlantic medal was denied the three ships. We had entered the war zone outside the set parameters for issue of the medal. Numerous approaches were made by senior members of both the Royal Navy and the Merchant Navy, but it was all to no avail and nothing was forthcoming. At the time it was a great disappointment as, war or not, the ships had been operating in very dangerous waters. 24 years on, however, it seems far less an issue than it was at the time.

RMS Centaur

Lady Elizabeth

Chapter 3

Ghost Ships of the South Atlantic

Shortly after our return to Rosyth, the *St Helena*, after a short refit, sailed once more for the Falklands to take up her new role as a mini troop/supply ship running between Ascension Island, Port Stanley and Grytviken, South Georgia.

I quickly settled down into what I hoped would be a long leave. Shortly afterwards, the *Centaur* which had been chartered by Curnow Shipping to fill the gap left by the *St Helena*, arrived in Avonmouth. I was requested to go along for the in-port stay to oversee the fitting of a teleprinter in the radio office. I was quite pleased about this as we had all heard so much about the magnificent *Centaur*, which it was hoped would replace the *St Helena* on a permanent basis. On arrival in Avonmouth, I found the ship to be very impressive, being almost three times larger than the *St Helena* and well over a hundred feet longer. Once aboard, however, I was to become greatly disappointed. As far as the public rooms and general arrangement was concerned, she was fine. Unfortunately, the radio office and radio officer's cabin were situated quite a long way from the bridge and were of very dismal aspect. The equipment was quite old and could not compare to that fitted aboard the *St Helena*. The situation was about to be improved by the fitting of a teleprinter, but this was unsuccessful. The communications engineer brought it aboard and commenced the installation with great confidence, but was never able to get it up and running. As I was only there in the capacity of an observer, my opinion was never asked as to what might have been the problem and tactful suggestions on my part were quickly dismissed. There was no guarantee that I would have succeeded either, but I really would have liked to try. Even the cabin was inferior to the one on the *St Helena*, and did not have its own bathroom, a luxury that I had grown accustomed to ever since joining the *Good Hope Castle* eight years previously.

The only Curnow staff sailing in the ship were the pursers and catering department as well as the deck and engine-room cadets. Prior to seeing the ship, I had asked if I might sail in her, but was turned down. After seeing it I was quite pleased that I was not to sail. While I was on board, I lived very comfortably in one of the passenger cabins; we had several social functions, so in general the stay was quite pleasant. The Curnow pursers thought the ship was excellent and assured me that she would soon be purchased and go into service on a permanent basis. Management did not seem so sure.

One thing surprised me. Most of the sea staff that had not gone south with the *St Helena* for various reasons seemed to take a great delight in stating 'After all that, you didn't do anything down there, it was all over when you arrived!' I found this attitude very hard to take indeed. We did not go down 'Hollywood style' to take on the Argentinian Army, Navy and Air Force with our four 20 mm guns. We went down to carry out the dangerous duties of mine clearance in the most appalling weather conditions and that task we had performed to the complete satisfaction of everyone. Eventually, the *Centaur* was ready to sail and I departed in the hope that she would not be purchased and I could return in due course to the *St Helena* which was where, I decided, I belonged.

A few days after Christmas, I was still looking forward to another couple of months leave when I received a telephone call from the office. It went something like this: 'Hello, Bob, how are you?' 'Fine, thanks, everything OK at your end?' 'Yes, great. Look would you do us a big favour and fly out to rejoin the ship at Ascension the day after tomorrow?' 'Eh, well…' 'Great Bob, thanks a million!' a click and the line went dead. I was unable to re-establish contact and the following morning a rail ticket to the RAF base at Lyneham turned up, telling me that I was to be flown out by Hercules transport the day after.

On arrival at the RAF base, I was allotted a room and told that my flight would be in the early hours of the following day. Ian Chessum, the 2nd officer had also arrived, he was flying out to join the big ferry *Rangatira* as 1st officer. Although the *Rangatira* was not a Curnow ship, head office had some reciprocal arrangement with them whereby the 1st officer and two catering officers were Curnow men. On the morning of the flight, John McMinn also arrived. Although he had been chief engineer while we were mine hunting, he was rejoining as 2nd engineer. This was simply because the normal chief, Brian Cooper, who had been too ill to go south with the ship was now recovered and had rejoined before she left the UK.

St Helena *with her funnel extension*

A single berth cabin

A comfortable lounge bar, complete with small dance floor, was provided for cabin passengers

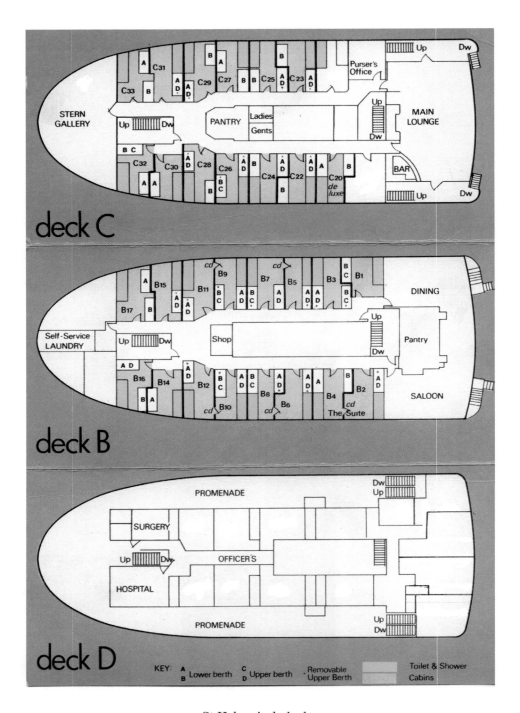

St Helena's *deck plan*

The 'Crossing the Line' ceremony

The swimming pool

The old passenger box

The holds are packed with everything the island needs

Comfortless Cove, Ascension Island

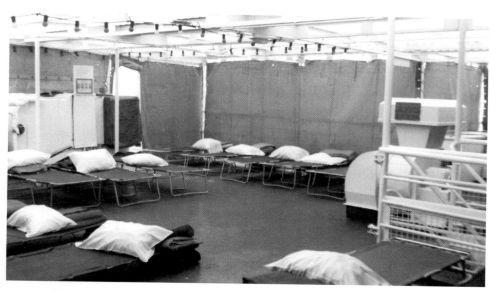

Deck passengers were carried between Ascension and St Helena in conditions reminiscent of the Conrad

St Helena *at Falmouth for restoration*

Overseas Argonaut
standing by

Fairplay IX
passing the tow rope

The author being hoisted off by Wessex helicopter

A blustery day in the Bay of Biscay

Louise *(formerly* Jennie S. Barker*)*

The small harbour at Tristan da Cunha

A typical dwelling on Tristan da Cunha

The new St Helena

The old St Helena *from the new ship*

Promenade of the new St Helena *at night*
(courtesy of St Helena Line)

Typical cabin on the new St Helena
(courtesy of St Helena Line)

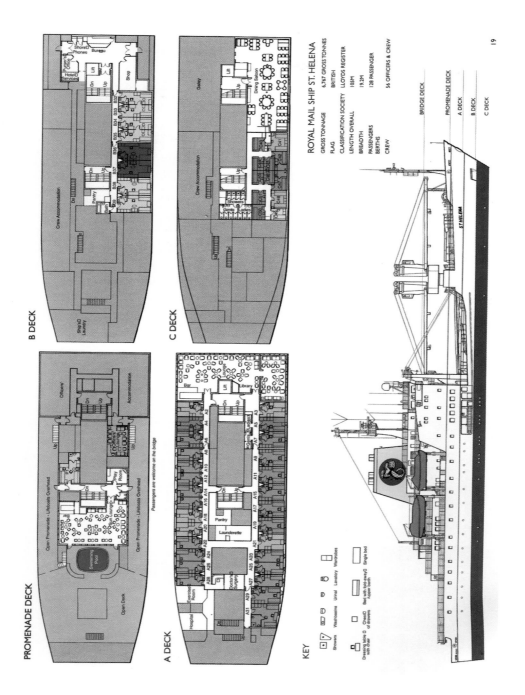

The profile and cabin plans of the new St Helena

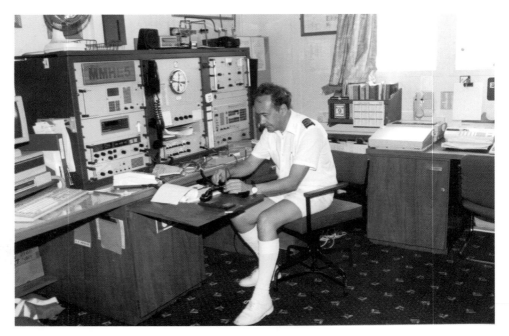

The author repairing a telephone in his last few days at sea, October 1992

St Helena, *old and new, at Cardiff*

Although I have never been all that keen on flying, the Hercules was quite an enjoyable experience. The main body of the aircraft was stacked up with cargo and luggage. The passengers which included a large number of service personnel as well as ourselves were simply packed round the sides of the cargo in very basic metal seats fitted with canvas covers. With most of them in camouflage greens, it looked like a scene from an old war movie as the great aircraft struggled into the sky, shaking and rattling and with the permanent scream of the engines ringing in our ears. I had anticipated the noise and purchased some very effective government surplus earmuffs before leaving home. Once airborne, we were left to ourselves and I followed the example of some of the others by climbing on top of the piles of luggage and stretching out full length. Because I was able to lie down, I found the flight considerably more comfortable than any of the airliners I had travelled on during my time with Silver Line. The only problem was the unremitting noise. We landed to refuel at Dakar in Senegal. We all had to leave the aircraft, but were not allowed into the terminal building on account of being military personnel. Instead we had to wait beside an open sewer in the stifling heat. Eventually, we touched down at Ascension Island. The old company tour bus collected us and drove us down to the pierhead where we found those whom we were relieving just coming ashore. I had time for a few words with Neil who, it transpired, was flying home for the birth of a second child. As we approached the *St Helena*, we could see that some changes had taken place. The helicopter hangar had been removed, but the flight deck remained. The guns had also been removed as well as the RAS derrick. When I had last seen the ship she was showing quite a lot of rust, but this had increased considerably and she had developed a very battered-looking appearance.

Once on board I found that everything, on the inside at least, seemed back to normal. The curtain separating the former RN wardroom from the petty officers was gone and everything was neat and tidy. The same had happened in the dining saloon and the ship seemed to have reverted to her normal passenger-carrying status again. I already knew most of the officers and crews, but there were one or two exceptions. Geoff, the purser, had been relieved by John Dimmock whom I knew quite well. He had been chief purser on the *Windsor Castle* most of the time I had been there. There were two new catering officers employed on a temporary basis. Angie Read, assistant purser, had dearly wanted to sail south with us on the mine hunting commission, but had not been allowed. She had, however, managed to return to the ship in our trooping/store ship role.

Most of the naval communications equipment had been removed. This included the container that had been situated down number four hold and quite a lot of the equipment had also been removed from my former cabin. I was not able to move back in as the satellite communications terminal remained. Once again, I was accommodated in the 3rd officer's cabin, while he occupied a passenger cabin lower down. The original radio office was back to normal with the lifting of radio silence.

As far as communications were concerned, things were not quite back to normal. The ship was still under Ministry of Defence charter and all the official communications had to be encrypted before transmission, while received traffic had to be decoded. An army corporal had been appointed to the ship to deal with this. He encrypted any message to be sent and simply handed me the rolled up punched paper tape for the teleprinter. It was my job to transmit it by satellite, although I had no idea of the content. Any messages received, came in automatically and he decoded them and handed them to the captain.

During our time with the navy, all satellite communications including coding and decoding had been carried out by the naval radio staff. Consequently, I had no idea how to use a satellite terminal. When I was given the first coded tape, I asked the corporal what the transmission procedure was. Initially, I got the rather militant reply that it was not his job to send messages, just to deal with the encrypting. I had to state firmly that I was not trying to order him to send them. I was asking politely how the equipment was operated. He then relented and showed me how it was done—it was very simple and we got on very well from then on.

The passage back to Port Stanley was easier the second time round. We were no longer subject to the naval exercises or confined to the tiny wardroom area. Even when the troops were aboard, both lounges were in full use. I asked one of the officers if it affected discipline in any way. He replied that it didn't: the fact that they were allowed to use the lounges at the same time as their officers seemed to be appreciated and they were all very well behaved.

On arrival at Port Stanley, the weather was much improved and considerably warmer. The snow had gone and it was possible to walk out on deck with a jacket and not feel cold. I was especially pleased to hear that I was no longer required to keep a bridge watch now that the navy had gone. This meant that as long as I had no equipment repairs or paperwork in hand, I was able to go ashore practically whenever I pleased while we were in harbour.

For many years I had wanted to visit the Falkland Islands in order to see the many wrecked sailing ships which littered the harbours and inlets. I had already managed to visit some of them during the previous commission, but bad weather and the difficulties in getting ashore prevented any in-depth study of the wrecks. With the aid of my Port Stanley wreck map, which I had obtained many years previously, I was able to locate and identify all of them. In most cases they were ships that had been mauled by the storms and seas off the infamous Cape Horn. Many of them, severely damaged, and leaking badly, had struggled towards the relative safety of the Falkland Islands. Many of them were found to be damaged beyond repair and were simply beached and left to rot. Others whose hulls were still fairly sound, but whose owners could not afford to pay for new masts and spars to be shipped out to them, were sold locally for use as storage hulks. It seems that no maintenance was done on the floating hulks, they were used until they wore out and then joined their more dilapidated sisters on the beaches and in the creeks and inlets. One very famous ship, Brunel's *Great Britain* was hulked in Port Stanley in 1886. At that time she was forty-two years old. After a further fifty-one years as a floating wool store in Port Stanley her condition was such that she was of no further use. The old ship was towed out of the harbour and beached in Sparrow Cove. On April 13th, 1937, several holes were cut below the waterline and the hulk of *Great Britain* settled into what was expected to be her final resting place. Thirty-three years later, however, the ancient ship received a reprieve and was brought home to Bristol for restoration. I had visited the ship a number of times while the *St Helena* was in Avonmouth and over the years watched as she was gradually restored to her original condition.

For many years I had been aware of the many shipwrecks around the Falkland Islands and ever since my schooldays had longed to visit the 'ghost ships of the South Atlantic'. With our mine clearance days behind us, I believed my chance had finally come.

Most of the wrecks that I was able to visit lay in Port Stanley Harbour itself. The largest and most impressive one was the iron barque *Lady Elizabeth* lying beached in Whalebone Cove at the eastern end of the harbour. She had been built at Sunderland in 1879 and had had an interesting career. Initially, she had been built for John Wilson, a London ship owner who named her *Lady Elizabeth*. It seems likely that the vessel was named after Elizabeth Wilson, John Wilson's mother. As far as I know I am not related to the original owner, but it would be nice to think so. Her first captain was Alexander Findlay, a sixty-year-old Scotsman. On the first voyage the *Lady Elizabeth* sailed from North Shields on the 11th September, 1879, with 1,760 tons of coal for Bombay. The coal freights in that year were between twenty-five and thirty shillings per ton. After discharge in Bombay she loaded at Madras for London. Arriving in the West India Dock, London on the 31st of October, she discharged a mixed cargo of jaggery, myrabolams, turmeric, nux vomica, redwood, goat and sheep skins, deer horns, hemp and hides. This cargo deserves some elaboration:

Jaggery .... sugar obtained by inspissation from palm sap;
Myrabolams .... fruit of a tropical tree used in dyeing and tanning;
Turmeric .... the root of an East Indian plant, 'curcuma longa',which
                 affords a yellow powder used as a dye;

Nux Vomica......... the fruit of a species of 'strychnos', from which strychnine is obtained.

On her second voyage, commencing in January 1881, she sailed from Middlesbrough to Reunion, probably with coal. She did not return to the UK until November 1883 when she arrived in London with 23,400 bags of rice loaded at Gopalpur. On the 13th of March, 1882, the *Lady Elizabeth* was in Mauritius. This was followed by a charter to Melbourne, Newcastle NSW, returning to Mauritius. After Mauritius she sailed north to India and loaded a cargo of rice for home.

By 1882, John Wilson was experiencing financial difficulties and he was forced to hand the *Lady Elizabeth* over to the bank. An iron barque is little use to a bank and in no time at all they sold the vessel to a Manx captain, George Christian Karran. Captain Karran kept the name *Lady Elizabeth*, but had her registered in Castletown, Isle of Man. The ship became home to Captain and Mrs Karran and their family for the next eight years. In 1884, the vessel encountered a hurricane and lost a number of sails. The front of the poop deck was also stove in and the accommodation flooded. Four years later, on the 3rd of May, 1888, Mrs Karran gave birth to their son Tom as the ship was sailing along the Chilean coast. In 1890, Captain Karran left the *Lady Elizabeth* to take command of the full-rigged ship *Manx King*. He finally retired in 1904.

By 1904, sail was on a very definite decline and after a special survey in that year, she was put up for sale. Early in the year 1906 she was sold to Nor-wegian owners who, like Captain Karran, also kept the name *Lady Elizabeth*. She sailed under the Nor-wegian flag for six years. Her sailing days finally came to an end in 1912. She had sailed from Delgoa Bay with a cargo of lumber. Off Cape Horn

On the deck of the Lady Elizabeth

the old ship received the severest beat-ing of her life. She received considerable damage on deck and four of her crew were washed overboard and drowned. Running for the safety of the Falkland Islands, she struck a rock off Volunteer Point and limped into Port Stanley the following day. A survey showed that the striking of the rock had set up and broken the keel of the ship, as well as punching a hole in the bottom. The *Lady Elizabeth* was then thirty-four-years old and beyond economic repair. She was condemned and sold for one thousand pounds. The hole was patched up and she served as a floating warehouse in Port Stanley Harbour until 1936. It was in that year that she dragged anchor and went ashore in Whalebone Cove. A hole was cut in the bottom to make sure she would remain where she was and then she was left to decay.

My first visit to the *Lady Elizabeth* was made during mine clearance operations in the dead of winter. Our lifeboat had been returning from one of the destroyers in Port William Sound. As we came in through the entrance it began to blow hard and quickly developed into a blizzard. Chief officer Chris Hughes was in charge of the boat and I suggested that we lay alongside the old barque in order to shelter until the weather moderated. The great rust-streaked hull was only a couple of hundred feet off and he quickly swung the tiller about and we came alongside just abreast of the mainmast. The old ship was canted towards us and the main-deck was only feet above the water. A battered looking ladder hung conveniently from one of the missing freeing ports. After tying the boat up we quickly climbed aboard. The three lower masts were still standing and the canted mainyard still creaked in its chain slings high above our heads. Initially we made for the shelter of the poop accommodation, which was gutted. All the cabin partitions had been knocked out forming a single large room which was littered with debris. Two circular iron stairways curved up to the poop deck and I gingerly ventured up one of them. The poop deck was practically bare. Most of the rails remained, but only a square mark in the deck planking showed where the charthouse had once stood, while a gaping hole was all that remained to show where the skylight had been. The steering mechanism remained intact, but the wheel had long since been removed by sawing through the spokes close to the boss. Moving along the main-deck, I entered the forward deckhouse. Here the cabins were still intact and even had the bunk frames in position. Part of the deckhouse was where the apprentices had lived, while a two-berth cabin was probably occupied by the bosun and carpenter. The forward part of the deckhouse was the galley. The whole structure was made of either iron or steel and was badly rusted with daylight showing through the deckhead.

The forecastle offered us the greatest protection from the elements. Although one iron door was hanging off its hinges, we were able to enter without any difficulty. Again, the frames of bunks were still arranged around the sides. The heel of the massive bowsprit extended well into this space; while aft of it was a huge rust-streaked windlass. In the days of sail, it was quite normal for the crew to share their accommodation with the windlass. This had two disadvantages. When the anchors were hove in, the chain cables which were often covered in stinking mud, passed through the hawse pipes into the forecastle, before going over the windlass sprockets and down into the chain locker below. As if this was not enough, the hawse pipes allowed access to wind and water when the ship was labouring in heavy seas. As we stood in the freezing cold of the forecastle looking out along the streaming main-deck, the old ship groaned and shifted slightly from time to time in the force of the wind. The ancient forecastle afforded us the same protection from the elements that it had offered to the ship's crew in her sailing days, but we were still cold and wet. It did not take much imagination to imagine what it must have been like for the seamen to clamber from sodden freezing bunks off Cape Horn. Out onto the flooded main-deck in the blackest of nights with the ship rolling and plunging. Climb onto the t'gallant rail and reach out for the icy steel shrouds and begin the ascent to the tops. Hanging backwards, they had to claw their way over the futtock shrouds and grope for the topmast rigging to pull themselves onto the top. Those whose work lay on the lower yards then had to step out onto the footropes slung beneath the yard and take a hold of the iron jackstay which ran along the top. Taking in the sail meant other seamen gathering it up by hauling on buntlines and clew lines on the deck far below. In a gale, the bunched sail would often inflate like a large canvas balloon, thrashing up and over the yard with the fury of the wind. Those sent aloft to furl, had to grab the canvas in handfuls and pull it down, trapping it beneath their bodies and the yard until the gaskets could be passed around the yard and the sail secured. Above the lower square sails, the *Lady Elizabeth* carried the lower topsails, upper topsails, single t'gallants and finally a royal on both the fore and mainmasts. The further up the seamen went, the greater the movement of the mast. The royals were about 150 feet above the deck. About nine years previously I had sailed briefly in a fifty-three-year-old three-masted topsail schooner and going aloft even in that small vessel had been a terrifying ordeal which I would never forget.

Eventually, the blizzard moderated and we returned to the comfort of the *St Helena*. Because of the weather and other pressing duties aboard our own ship, I was not able to make a second visit to the ship until our second phase of Falklands duty began. By this time, the weather was much better and I was able to visit the ship a number of times. On one occasion the weather was actually bordering on mild and the sun shone brilliantly. I was able to descend the iron ladder set in the coaming of number three hatch. The lower holds were flooded to just below the tweendecks. Although the tweendeck planking had been stripped, the iron beams remained and I was able to walk along the full length of the ship on the remaining ironwork. As I passed the mainmast, I could see the heel of it set firmly in the keelson as the whole scene was illuminated by sunlight which shone in through a fairly large hole below the waterline. The water within the hull was lit to a brilliant turquoise and the scene was one of strange beauty. When I reached the forepeak, I could see down into the chain locker, where the anchor cables lay in huge coils where they had been flaked down over half a century before. In several places, the iron hull plating had split and opened, leaving cracks about an inch wide. In later years I heard of a number of plans to restore the old ship, and even to sail her again. This, I feel, would be impossible: although the hull appears to be in one piece, the iron has corroded through in a number of places and the keel was broken when she struck rocks making for Port Stanley some seventy years ago.

The next four wrecks are more accessible and lie grouped around the Falkland Islands Company jetty. They are the Welsh brig *Fleetwing*, the Canadian barque *Egeria*, the American clipper *Snowsquall* and the British barque *William Shand*.

The *Fleetwing* lies along the shingle beach and we were able to step aboard without even getting our feet wet. This small wooden vessel had been built at Porthmadog, Wales, in 1874. With a tonnage of only 242, she was a mere 107 feet in length with a beam of 25 feet. Her original rig was that of a brig, two masts with square sails on both of them. This vessel is unusual amongst the other Port Stanley hulks because she arrived on purpose and not seeking shelter after storm damage. She was initially commanded by Captain Owen Jones, then aged 26. For such a small vessel, the voyages were amazingly long and varied. She ventured to Naples, Girgenti, Oporto, Szczecin, Dakar, Buenos Aires, Rosario, Cape Town and Demerara. At one time she was employed carrying slate to the Baltic and the Elbe. In 1887, the *Fleetwing* left Newport, Wales, for Santa Caterina, Brazil. They arrived on the 31st October, 1887, and then went on to New York, Natal and Hamburg. They arrived in Middles-borough a few days before Christmas 1888. The voyage had taken sixteen months!

A Captain Griffiths then took command of the brig. For the next three years she sailed in the South American phosphate and nitrate trade. In 1893, Captain Griffiths left to take command of the splendid new steel barque *Beeswing*. From 1893 until 1903, the *Fleetwing* was commanded by Captain Pritchard. By 1898, the twenty-four-year-old ship was showing signs of age and was given a very thorough refit. This included a new keel and deck. The *Fleetwing* continued to operate successfully in international waters until 1911 when her owners decided to sell her. The thirty-seven-year-old vessel was purchased by a company in Port Stanley. With a Liverpool crew and under the command of Captain J. D. Parsell, of Bootle, the old brig sailed from Liverpool towards the Falkland Islands. That

Fleetwing

was in mid July 1911. After an uneventful passage, the *Fleetwing* arrived in Port Stanley on the 30th October 1911 and was delivered to her new owners in a shipshape and seaworthy state.

Despite the fact that the old brig was still sound, the new owners removed the masts and rigging and first used her as a barge and later as a storage hulk for wool. Eventually, she was beached and abandoned, her final role being that of a rubbish tip. In 1982 she presented a sorry picture. The deck had gone and the empty hull was being used as a dump for a large number of empty forty-gallon oil drums. It was hard to imagine her as the trim little brig that she had once been. It was even harder to believe that such a tiny ship could have sailed on such extensive voyages, as far afield as the Pacific, for so many years without accident or mishap. She was a credit to her Welsh builders and the seamen of Porthmadog who had sailed her for so long in such a professional manner that she never came to any harm or was involved in any untoward incident.

Slightly ahead of the *Fleetwing* lies the remnants of the last American clipper in existence, the *Snowsquall*. This ship was built in 1851 by A. Butler at Cape Elizabeth for Charles R. Green of New York. This 742-ton full-rigged ship arrived in Port Stanley on March 2nd, 1864. She was under the command of Captain Dillingham and was 59 days out of Philadelphia heading towards San Francisco with general cargo and an undisclosed amount of gunpowder. She had been driven ashore in the Straits of Le Maire and had sustained damage to the rudder and bottom planking. At Port Stanley, she was considered to be beyond economical repair and was purchased by the Falkland Islands Company for use as a store hulk. By the time I visited her, she had deteriorated to the extent that only about twenty feet of the forward part remained above water. I was able to climb aboard and see the extremely fine lines of the forward hull. Towards the end of our time in the Falklands, researchers from the Peabody Museum, Salem, USA were surveying the wreck with a view to removing the forward section and re-assembling it in Salem.

The *Snowsquall* had a lucky escape from destruction during the American Civil War. While rounding the Cape of Good Hope, they encountered another ship which was flying the American flag. The two ships eventually became close enough for crew members to shout across. Suddenly, the Stars and Stripes flown by the other ship came down at a run and, to the horror of all aboard *Snowsquall*, the new flag which broke out at the gaff was that of the Confederate States of America! As Captain Dillingham ordered the *Snowsquall* to be put about to a better point of sailing, a row of gunports opened along the side of the other ship. Sail after sail was piled on the *Snowsquall*'s straining masts and yards as she strove to get clear of the confederate raider. Fortunately, the rebel (CSS *Tuscaloosa*) could not match the sailing qualities of the *Snowsquall* and by nightfall she was out of danger.*

Alongside a nearby jetty, fifty feet or so away from the *Snowsquall* lies the remains of the big 1,006-ton wooden barque *Egeria*. This vessel arrived in Port Stanley on September 12th, 1872, 95 days out from London on passage towards Callao with a cargo of coal. She was under the command of Captain Matthew Henry Foster. Where she sustained the damage that drove her to seek refuge in the Falklands is not known, but like so many others, she was condemned on arrival and scuttled alongside a jetty. Only the stern section remained in 1982,

---

* On 20th June, 1863, the Confederate State Cruiser Alabama, under the command of Captain Raphael Semmes, captured the 500-ton American barque Conrad, which was en route from Buenos Aires to New York with a cargo of goat skins and wool. Captain Semmes immediately renamed the vessel Tuscaloosa and fitted her with three of Alabama's 12-pounder guns and transferred 15 of the Alabama's men to crew her under the command of Lt J. Low to operate as a Confederate Cruiser in South African waters. After a relatively short cruise, the Tuscaloosa was seized by the British authorities in Simon's Bay, South Africa, on Boxing Day, 1863. She was finally released to her owners in March, 1864.

but it was still in everyday use. The ship had been cut off at the break of the poop and the open end planked over. Another jetty had been extended past the cut-off section and access to the hulk was gained through a small door. Visiting the wreck with Captain Smith, we decided to have a look inside. We opened the door and stepped inside to find it full of dockers. On seeing us, they all stood up and remained standing as we inspected the interior of the ship. All the accommodation and fittings had been removed and it appeared as an immensely strong wooden warehouse. As we left, they all sat down again. Who they thought we were, we never really figured out—we were not in uniform. Captain Smith had a yachting cap on and I had a lumberjack hat with a Merchant Navy badge sewn on the front, which, we presumed, had made them think we were Royal Navy.

Not far from the remains of the *Egeria*, lay the fast dwindling remains of another ancient. This was the 432-ton British barque *William Shand*, which had been built at Greenock, Scotland in 1839. The *William Shand* first arrived in Port Stanley in a damaged condition on the 1st February, 1859. She was under the command of Captain Waller and was on passage from Liverpool towards Valparaiso with a cargo of coal. She had a crew of nineteen and had been at sea

Egeria *(only the stern remains)*

for 98 days since leaving Liverpool. Repairs were completed in just over two weeks and she set out once again for Valparaiso. Once again, she received a battering off Cape Horn and after two months trying to weather the Cape, severe damage forced her to run for the Falklands again. This time, however, the ship was beyond economical repair and was condemned and purch-ased by the Falkland Islands Company for use as a storage hulk.Unfortunately, the heavy harbour traffic of the Task Force took a heavy toll on the old ship and by the time I was able to make a visit, she was rapidly being reduced to matchwood!

Further up the harbour, opposite the town lie two more wrecks. The oldest one, the *Actaeon* lies closest to the shore. This vessel was a 561-ton barque built at Miramichi, New Brunswick, in 1838. The history of the *Actaeon* is virtually unknown. She arrived at Port Stanley on January 27th, 1853. She had been badly damaged off Cape Horn after a long and trying passage from Liverpool towards San Francisco. When she arrived, she was 154 days out of Liverpool. She was the first vessel to be scuttled at the end of West Jetty. Over the years she settled into the mud and became unusable.

Next to the *Actaeon* lies the hulk of the American ship *Charles Cooper*. This 850-ton barque was built at Boston, USA, starting her maiden voyage from New York in 1856. She arrived at Port Stanley on September 25th, 1866. At that time she was 92 days out of Liverpool en route towards Melbourne with a cargo of coal. After receiving damage off the Horn, she ran for the Falklands where she was subsequently condemned. For four years the ship was used as a floating storage hulk, but was scuttled alongside the *Actaeon* in 1870. The jetty was then extended through the now disused *Actaeon* hulk into the *Charles Cooper*.

In 1982, the *Actaeon* was very low in the water, while the *Charles Cooper* still towered above her bolt upright and with every appearance of still being afloat. Closer inspection, however, showed that she was firmly on the bottom and a large amount of the hull planking on and below the waterline was gone. A ramshackle warehouse-style roof had, at some time, been erected over the *Charles Cooper*, hiding her deck arrangement. Unfortunately, the jetty leading out to the two hulks had been partially destroyed and I was never able to get aboard either ship. Consequently I had to satisfy myself with observing them from our boat when coming and going from the various jetties. The planking of the *Charles Cooper* appeared to be quite sound above the waterline, but the hull had been weakened by a huge square access hole being cut in the seaward side In 1968, the South Street Seaport Museum in New York bought the *Charles Cooper*. Between 1976 and 1981 a number of experts were sent out from America to stabilise the hull. Whether or not they intended to try and move the ship to New York, I do not know. In 1991, however, the American owners transferred the responsibility of the hulk to the Falkland Islands government. From that time the remains continued to deteriorate unchecked. Eventually *Charles Cooper* collapsed into the harbour and became a menace to harbour traffic; the remains were recently lifted out with a crane and put on the shore.

The hulk of the old wooden ship *Jhelum* lay alongside a very rickety wooden jetty opposite the governor's residence. She was launched at Liverpool in 1849 from the yard of Joseph Steel & Son. Initially she was a full-rigged ship. The hull was largely constructed of mahogany. The hull was decorated by ten painted 'gunports' on either side. These were mainly for decoration, but they could serve a useful purpose by giving the ship an appearance of a navy frigate and so deter any pirates thinking of attacking them. The *Jhelum* was only a small vessel with a length of 128 feet and a tonnage of 428. In 1858 she was cut down to a barque by removing the square sails from the mizzen mast leaving only the spanker and a gaff topsail. On July 13th, 1870, she sailed from Callao, Peru, with a cargo of guano. Her destination was Dunkirk, but she had a bad time of it rounding the Horn and put in to Port Stanley on the 18th August, 1870, in order to repair a leak that had developed. Once in the safety of the harbour, the crew refused to sail and the ship was condemned. She was scuttled close to the beach and used as a store for petroleum products. After many years in that capacity, she fell into disrepair and was left to rot. Despite over a hundred years of neglect, the *Jhelum* was still holding together in 1982 and was regarded as one of the best surviving examples of this type of ship. All of the deck forward of the poop had gone, although a number of deck beams remained. The big anchor windlass had fallen through into the hold and was lying in the bottom of the ship. The area of the poop had been roofed over with corrugated iron at some stage. This had protected the decking and so the accommodation still afforded some protection against the elements. The captain's cabin was quite large with stern windows looking aft. All the furnishings had long gone. At the forward end of the poop were two very small partitioned areas which I assume were the officer's cabins. Below the main cabin, a huge iron water tank could still be seen. The hull of the *Jhelum* is now badly twisted and warped, but still relatively complete. The construction is quite massive: the frames and deck beams are held together by large forged iron straps bolted in position. Since 1982, the jetty has been demolished making access more difficult.

Moving further along the shore, the remains of the 615-ton barque *Margaret* lie beneath the government jetty. Not a great deal is known about this ship. She arrived in Port Stanley late in the year 1850 while en-route from Liverpool towards Valparaiso with a cargo of coal and cannon balls. Under the command of Captain D. Till, the ship had been at sea for about 200 days. Two months of this time were spent trying to get around Cape Horn. Finally, the overloaded ship began to leak and she was forced to run for the Falklands. She was surveyed

Jhelum

Jhelum *(the captain's cabin looking forward)*

and subsequently condemned on arrival. For many years she was used as a coal hulk in the harbour until she was too worn out for further service. She was then scuttled and the jetty built over the top. It is was difficult to distinguish wreck from jetty in 1982. Some of the frames and side planking were visible when approaching in a boat, but it was not immediately apparent that the structure was ever a ship. On a bright sunny afternoon, I was able to look beneath the jetty from our boat. The whole of the hull appeared to be full of rubble. What I took to be the sternpost, projected up through the jetty and was used as a mooring post for the numerous small boats that in 1982 were constantly coming and going. A number of feet forward of the sternpost, I could make out the round stump of the mizzen mast, but this was cut off below the level of the jetty.

At the western end of the harbour lies the remains of the barque *Capricorn*. This vessel is very old, having been built at Swansea in 1829. Of only 380 tons, the *Capricorn* led an uneventful life for over fifty years. In February 1882, she was beached and scuttled on Tierra del Fuego in order to extinguish a serious fire in her cargo of coal. Once the fire was out, temporary repairs were made and the ship sailed to Port Stanley in the hope of repair. On arrival, however, she was condemned and subsequently sold to J. M. Dean & Sons for use as a storage hulk. She remained with them until 1889 when she was transferred to the Falkland Islands Company, also for use as a storage hulk. Eventually, in the 1940s, the *Capricorn* sank at her moorings. In 1942 she was pumped out and beached in her present position. A small jetty was built connecting her to the shore. Firmly on the bottom, the ancient ship then carried on as a storage hulk for a number of years. Eventually, her condition deteriorated to the extent that she was finally abandoned . The upper parts of the hull were soon taken away for use as firewood. In 1982, only the stem and stern posts and a row of broken frames remained above water.

This concludes my survey of the sailing ship wrecks in Port Stanley harbour. There were more to be found in Grytviken, South Georgia, but I will come to them presently.

Our new employment as a stores ship/mini troop carrier meant that we were spending far less time at anchor than during the mine clearance operations. On completion of discharge, we would sail back up to Ascension Island to load cargo. Our passenger accommodation was normally filled with a mixture of Royal Air Force, Army or Government officials. As a result, we were back again to our normal role of being a passenger/cargo liner. The main difference was that our passengers were all travelling in official capacities at someone else's expense. Consequently they were far less demanding than our normal passengers. As long as they had the use of the bar, shop and public rooms with regular films or bingo sessions everyone was happy—the majority regarded it as an unexpected bonus. Although we carried on wearing uniform, it was no longer thought necessary to dress for dinner in the evenings and everything became comfortable and relaxed. Entertainments such as dances, fancy dress evenings etc. were not considered applicable to members of the armed forces, so they were discontinued. I found life very acceptable on our new run. My army corporal assistant was quickly replaced by an amiable RAF sergeant, Brian Aspinwall, who was nearing retirement. He had been 'borrowed' from the big liner *Rangatira* which had become an almost a permanent feature of Port Stanley Harbour since the islands were recaptured. He fitted in well with the ship's officers and crew and Captain Smith decided that as he and his encrypting machine seemed to have become a permanent fixture in the radio office, he may as well be awarded an 'honorary' status of 2nd radio officer. He was given his own cabin and dined with the officers in the saloon.

Although radio silence had been lifted, I was not particularly overworked. All the official communications went via the satellite and Brian took the brunt of these as he was the only one allowed to use the encrypting machine. Sending the encoded messages was a simple matter of 'button pushing.' I found that few of our service passengers bothered communicating very much, so my job had settled down to a very comfortable level. The quality of the food was not quite as good as before, but this was simply due to the fact that it was much more difficult to obtain. One thing most of the servicemen really enjoyed was chocolate! After one stores flight from the UK arrived, Geoff the purser showed me an entire passenger cabin full to the doorway with cases of Mars Bars.

It was pleasant to get away from the cold and up to the warmth of Ascension on a regular basis. Never much of an enthusiast about flying, I settled down to remaining with the ship until our eventual return to the UK. In truth, I was enjoying the new run and was quite happy to remain, but as we headed north in late March, 1983, the company advised me that Neil would be relieving me in Ascension. When we arrived, Harry the cook and myself were told that we were to be lifted off by helicopter. I was the first to go. With a huge Wessex helicopter hovering above the flight deck, I went out and stood directly beneath it with instructions to 'do nothing'. As I stood there in the fierce downdraught, a wire line with a loop on the end was lowered down. The flight deck officer placed it over my head and under my arms. He then forgot to pull the clip down tightening the loop around me. The winch man then hauled me up. It was not a particularly frightening experience, but it was extremely uncomfortable and I felt myself gradually slipping as the clip was not pulled down. Once up to the door, the crewman grabbed me by the harness and dumped me on the floor holding me there with his foot while he secured the wire. He then lifted me up, spun me round and took the loop off before depositing me on the floor again. After making sure I was well away from the door, he hauled Harry up in a similar manner. Our luggage followed and we were flown straight to the airfield. The photograph of me being hoisted off was given to me on my return to the ship.

Our flight to the UK was to be in a conventional RAF airliner. Take-off was quite unnerving as the wing tips seemed to be almost touching the mounds of hardened lava on either side of the runway. Once we were in the air, we all settled down to a comfortable flight home. Later in the morning, an RAF stewardess gave us all a cup of tea. We had both found the sugar and milk sachets earlier and duly put them in and stirred it up. Mine tasted awful. Harry agreed and said it tasted as if they hadn't washed the cups for a month! As the stewardess came to take the empty cups away she said with smile 'And how's the Merchant Navy getting on then?' 'OK' replied Harry, 'How did you know we were Merchant Navy?' 'Nobody else would put sugar and milk in their beef tea!' she said and went off grinning.

After one month at home, I was told to rejoin the *St Helena* at Ascension Island. Several of us were to be flown out from Brize Norton by the RAF. I was pleased to be able to get a seat next to the emergency exit which provided twice as much space as the normal seats. We took off normally and all went well until we were passing over Gibraltar. The captain then came on the public address system with the news that the aircraft had developed technical problems and was to return to Brize Norton. This was met by both concern and annoyance. If there was something wrong with the aircraft, why could we not land at Gibraltar? We were informed that the problem lay in the radio equipment. The flight back was generally without incident although I felt that we were rattling and behaving slightly erratically. This may well have been my imagination, but my companions, including Brian Cooper chief engineer, also had similar misgivings. As we approached the UK we were advised that the aircraft was going to jettison some unused fuel and that we were not to be alarmed. All the information served to do was make us more nervous. In due course we arrived at the airfield and landed without incident. Once on the ground, the doors were flung open and we were told to get out as quickly as possible and run for the terminal building. We needed no urging and the aircraft was soon evacuated. As it stood on the runway, there were no visible signs that there was anything wrong with it. In our ignorance, we expected to board another aircraft and set off almost immediately, but we were informed that we would have to wait until the radio was repaired and then re-board the same aircraft. So, the long wait began. We noticed that the engine cowlings were all opened up as the maintenance teams set to work inside them, which brought the obvious comments that they kept their radio equipment in strange places! After several hours, the cowlings were closed and the maintenance staff departed. As the fuelling tanker approached, a tremendous thunderstorm began and the tanker withdrew. We would have to wait until the storm was over as fuelling was not permitted during electrical storms! It went on and on and it was not until very late in the evening that we took off again. This time we were crammed into the normal seats as others had got the best seats around the emergency exit. This time, the flight went without a hitch and we landed at Ascension Island in the early hours.

Once we were out of the aircraft, everyone else was quickly collected and taken away to their various billets. The few of us from the *St Helena*, however, seemed to have been forgotten about. We were none too pleased to be told that there wasn't a ship by the name of *St Helena* at the anchorage anyway! The RAF officer in charge then telephoned Mike Underwood to come and collect us. Mike was a Curnow chief officer who had been looking after the company's interest in Ascension during our MOD service, and we had three ships, the *Centaur*, the *Aragonite* and the *St Helena* calling at the island on a regular basis. (Normally Cable & Wireless acted as our agents.)

In a few minutes, Mike arrived with the astounding news that no one had told him we were coming and that the ship wasn't due to arrive until the following day! He added that he only had one spare bed at his bungalow. Brian Cooper, the chief engineer, was the senior, so he wisely said that he would take it and off they went. The RAF officer then contacted the Army and asked if we could be accommodated at 'Concertina City.' Following the recapture of the Falklands Islands, a lot of British military personnel passed through Ascension Island on the way to and from the Falklands. The sleepy backwater had become a hive of bustling activity. In order to accommodate vast numbers of men, a number of huge living containers had been sent out from Britain for use on the island. These containers were made from some soft material similar to heavy cardboard. They arrived squashed down rather like a concertina squeezebox. Once in position, they were stretched out to their full length. Each one was a similar size to the metal containers often seen on lorries travelling to and from the docks. They were fully air conditioned and fitted with rows of beds, functional, but not particularly comfortable. The group of prefabs quickly became known as 'Concertina City'.

After about an hour on the airfield, we were taken to one of these prefabs and allotted beds. Because of the air conditioning, it was freezing cold inside, despite the heat of Ascension. The following morning we had a look at the primitive facilities that the servicemen had to endure. A big communal shower area was provided which we made use of, but the toilet facilities left a lot to be desired. As far as I can remember, a fairly large warehouse had been taken over for this purpose. Around the inside were four rows of standard toilet bowls set in about four feet from the walls. They were all connected by a single waste disposal pipe and what appeared to be a permanent flush system. There was not even a pretence at privacy. Having taken one look at this area, we decided to search elsewhere. We made immediately for the American Base where we found our transatlantic cousins living in a fair degree of comfort. We were greeted enthusiastically and made most welcome. We did not bother returning to Concertina City, but took lunch with the Americans. Then we went down to Georgetown and established ourselves in the 'Exiles Club', where we remained until the eventual arrival of a very battered and rusty looking *St Helena* later that day. Never was a sight more welcome and it was with great relief that we climbed the scarred sides onto the rusty, but welcoming deck.

We were soon on our way south again and in due course arrived in Port Stanley. During our time in Port Stanley, we often entertained guests aboard. Amongst these was Lord Shackleton son of the great explorer Ernest Shackleton. He came aboard for dinner one evening and despite his advancing years, had no problem negotiating the pilot ladder which was our normal means of access. He was a lively and entertaining man and we all enjoyed his visit. I had met him 29 years previously when he had given a talk about Antarctic exploration at my school in Preston. I remember being fascinated by his stories and when he signed my autograph book I never dreamed that I would meet him again so many years later in Port Stanley.

As well as sailing regularly up to Ascension Island, we also made a number of crossings to Grytviken South Georgia to relieve the small British garrison which had been established there. On one of these calls, we took the Irish Rangers across and during the passage the ship began to vibrate and bounce in an alarming manner. The weather was calm and certainly should not have caused the unusual movement. A telephone call to the engine room revealed that all was well with the engine, but they also were suffering from the strange movement. It took about twenty minutes to discover the reason: the soldiers had been assembled on the flight deck and were being put through a series of physical exercises which required them all to jump up and down in unison with arms flapping out and down as they did so. Their combined weight was having a very adverse effect on the 3,000-ton ship. When they were asked to stop the vibration ceased immediately.

As we drew closer to Grytviken, the weather became icy cold again and we sighted about fourteen or fifteen huge icebergs, some of them apparently making a fair speed in the wind. These were the first bergs I had seen since Captain Neal pointed one out to me in the darkness of the North Atlantic aboard the *Joya McCance* 21 years earlier. In daylight they were majestic sights and we were all impressed with the awesome beauty of them. At the junction with the water they almost glowed with the most beautiful translucent turquoise which

I have never seen truly captured on camera. One of the icebergs sighted was approximately 700 feet in length, 100 feet wide and 145 feet high. It contained an estimated 1.3 million tons of ice. The *St Helena* passed it at a safe distance of 24 miles.

Arrival mornings at South Georgia were picturesque in the extreme. Even at a great distance, there seemed to be snow-covered mountains and giant glaciers everywhere. On the visit in question, we approached just as it was becoming light. The air was clear and everything stood out in sharp focus and appeared almost in black and white. As we approached the headland, a piper stood on the bridge top began playing the bagpipes. As we came round into King Edward Cove we saw a number of men hurrying out of the various buildings to see a very rusty and battered looking ship arriving to the sound of the pipes. We crossed the cove and lay alongside the rickety jetty of the old whaling station. With the morning sunlit, the true beauty of the scene was upon us. On three sides we had the towering mountains with snow blowing off the highest peaks, while to seaward there were more snow-covered mountains in the distance. Close to the jetty was the abandoned whaling station consisting of a large number of buildings, oil tanks and chimneys. There was even a picturesque church set slightly aside from the town. Everywhere was a scene of aban-doned dereliction. Close by the ship were two half-sunk steam whale catchers, while further along

Shackleton's grave at Grytviken

another one remained afloat. The top of the old floating dry-dock could be seen where it had settled on the bottom of the harbour after years of neglect. On the other side of the cove, the massive wooden hulk of an old American sailing ship lay beached on the snow-covered shore.

We were to remain alongside for two days and I had plenty of time to explore. Captain Smith and myself climbed to the top of one of the smaller hills and it was from that vantage point that I took the photograph showing the ship, the whaling station and the mountains. The stump of the bowsprit of the sailing ship hulk points directly to the small graveyard where the remains of Ernest Shackleton lie. It is just discernable above the small white building to the right of the hulk.

On the end of the jetty, towards the stern of the *St Helena*, lay two partly submerged wrecks. These were the steam whale-catchers *Albatross* and *Dias*. The *Albatross* lay alongside the jetty with the *Dias* next to her. Both vessels were lying on the bottom and canted over with their upperworks above the sea. We were unable to board them because of the danger of falling into the icy water. In the 1950s when the whaling station was still in operation there were a number of small vessels named *Albatross* in the Lloyds register. Most likely, the one

The whale-catchers Albatross *and* Dias

lying in Grytviken is the one listed as being built in 1921 at Svelvik, She was 210 gross tons with a length of 11 feet and a breadth of 21.5 feet. *Dias* is shown as being built at Beverley, England by Cook, Welton & Gemmell in 1906 as a steam trawler. Her original name was *Viola*, later *Kapduen* and finally *Dias*. She was 167 gross tons with a length of 108.5 feet and a beam of 21.5 feet.

Further around the cove and almost opposite the flensing deck of the whale station, lay a third catcher. This was the *Petrel*, listed as being built at Oslo in 1928. She was the largest of the three, with a gross tonnage of 248. Her length was 122.5 feet and she had a beam of 23 feet. Unlike the other two, the *Petrel* was still afloat. She was loosely moored and lay about three feet off the jetty when we arrived. Three feet does not seem a long way, but when there is snow and ice about with freezing water below, the gap looked quite large. Eventually, we plucked up courage and jumped across. The ship had been completely gutted of all furniture and fittings. The cabins were empty shells strewn with rubbish. The bridge had also been cleaned out and although a rusty radar scanner was mounted on top of the lattice mast, the equipment itself had long gone. Down in the engine room, we found that over the decades of dereliction she had begun to take on water. It had almost reached the level of the open furnace doors.

From my point of view, the most interesting wreck in the cove was the huge wooden sailing ship *Louise*. I was able to discover very little about her other than the fact that her original name had been *Jennie S. Barker* and she had been built in the USA in the 1860s. She had arrived at Grytviken in the early years of the 20th century for use as a storage hulk. The bow was actually on the beach, but the stern was still in fairly deep water, but certainly resting on the bottom. The bowsprit had been sawn off short at some time. Although the hull was wooden, the remaining fore lower mast was iron. This was canted over slightly and held up by two steel wires. One of them led from the foretop down to the starboard side of the ship, the other to the stump of the bowsprit. The whole thing looked rather precarious and I have no doubt that if anyone cast either of the wires off, the mast would go over the side. We could not get aboard from the shore as the flared bow towered high above our heads. We then decided to go alongside the stern of the wreck in the ship's boat. We came alongside the starboard quarter and made fast. The wooden hull was so rotten that we were able to kick footholes in it as we went up the side. Once on board we looked upon a scene of utter shambles and decay. Over ninety per cent of the main deck and tween deck had gone, leaving a number of rotted beams spanning the holds. The holds were decaying pits into which we dared not venture. The ship had apparently been used as a rubbish dump and the holds contained what appeared to be thousands of empty bottles of all shapes and sizes. Despite the advanced decay, the sides of the ship were very thick and although spongy underfoot, we were able to walk carefully to the bows. The forecastle deck had partially collapsed, so we were unable to gain entrance. Aft of the forecastle lay the huge barrel of the windlass, still with two turns of wire around one of the drums. Again, we dared not venture too close to the windlass as it seemed poised to go crashing through into the hold at any moment! Several doors had been cut in the bows above the waterline. These were known as 'timber ports'. Towards the end of commercial sail, old wooden ships often took cargoes of lumber. The ports were cut in the bows in order to feed long lengths of timber into the holds. They were then sealed up until the ship arrived in its next port. They did tend to deface and even weaken the hull, but windjammers could not pick and choose their cargo during the final era of sail. The *Jennie S. Barker*, although in the final stages of decay was still an imposing sight when the towering bows were viewed from the beach.

The final wreck was more modern. Some way off the shore we found the listing hull of the Argentinian submarine *Santa Fe*, the conning tower bearing the scars of missile strikes. The bows were tilted slightly upwards and the name *Santa Fe* was clearly visible on the black plating. The wreck was strictly 'out of bounds' and we had to content ourselves with sailing past in the lifeboat.

Petrel *at Grytviken*

During one of our calls, Geoff the purser decided to put a pantomime on for the troops, thus claiming the most southern showing of *Cinderella* on record. The stage was built up in the forward lounge from cases of beer. All the parts were taken by MN officers. The starring roles went to Stuart, our young second officer who, like it or not, was given the part of Cinders. Geoff, dressed in a scruffy pair of long-johns was a very odd-looking Prince Charming, while Brian Cooper took his usual role as a bearded fairy godmother. The evening was a tremendous success with lots of cheers and cat calls and wolf whistles from the troops. When the Irish Rangers discovered that the stage was made from cases of beer, they started drinking it! To cap it all, a heavy gale blew up in the middle of the night and all hands were called at short notice to secure the ship.

About the time we left Grytviken in May 1983, the Ministry of Defence ordered us to return to Port Stanley to discharge stores and equipment and then proceed home to the Harland and Wolff ship yard at Belfast, Northern Ireland for restoration. This was welcome news indeed as the ship was beginning to feel the effects of the past year quite badly. Number one hatch in particular was giving trouble. With the constant opening and closing, plus the prolonged battering from heavy seas coming aboard, it was beginning to leak rather badly. On one

Louise's windlass

Santa Fe

occasion when it was opened, the hold was half full of icy water with the cargo floating about in it above the tweendeck level. The ship was never in danger of sinking, but the increasing ingress of water through the hatch cover was causing concern.

On completion of discharge, we sailed from Port Stanley with our passenger accommodation empty and made a leisurely passage up to Ascension Island. The ship seemed unusually quiet without passengers and the normally large catering and hotel services staff on board. I was really looking forward to the refit at Harland and Wolff, in the hope of gaining access to their collection of ship plans dating back to the nineteenth century. Curnow Shipping, however, had other ideas. With the head office being at Helston, Cornwall, they did not particularly like the idea of the ship being refitted so far away. Eventually, they were able to persuade the Ministry of Defence to send the ship to the ship repair yard at Falmouth, which was a lot more convenient. And so on a bright sunny afternoon, the battered and dejected looking *St Helena* crept alongside one of the lay-up berths and quietly 'went to sleep,' after a long and arduous MOD charter which had lasted just over a year.

Chapter 4

St Helena Swansong

Our arrival at Falmouth caused a tremendous change to our general way of life. We were to enjoy a very fine, hot summer alongside a clean and pleasant lay-up berth. A large number of workmen descended on the ship and set about restoring it and repairing all the damage that it had sustained during the year in the hostile South Atlantic. The ship was dry-docked, shot-blasted and repainted. Sections of the bulwarks were renewed where we had suffered a glancing blow from a tanker while going alongside in bad weather. All the military equipment, including the satellite communications system, was removed and my cabin was completely refurbished. Number one hatch cover was found to be so badly damaged that it had to be replaced. The new hatch had a raised coaming and stout new steel hatch covers.

The ship repairers did a fine job and nothing was overlooked. When restoration was finally complete, we were told that we were to remain laid up in Falmouth with a skeleton crew. This was because the *Centaur* and *Aragonite* were still on the St Helena run and would be for some time. I thought that I may be sent home on leave after we arrived. On telephoning Neil, however, he said that as we were not expected back so soon, his parents were flying out from New Zealand for a visit and would I mind staying with the ship. This I agreed to do as the weather was fine and we were in pleasant surroundings. Our new life of leisure consisted of breakfast in the saloon followed by a buffet lunch in the forward lounge. The evening meal was served about 1700 hours in order to allow the catering staff to make the most of their stay in Falmouth.

In the evenings, most of the ship's company would go off in small groups either to eat out, visit the cinema or frequent the many comfortable public houses which abounded in Falmouth. My companions in the evenings were generally Captain Bob Wyatt and Glenda, the stewardess. We usually set off walking shortly after the meal and had one or two drinks in a pub or hotel and then walk on to another. In this way we got a lot of exercise, did not drink too much and never ended up with hangovers. Sometimes we would go out for an evening meal in style and at the weekends we would venture further afield by car.

Once the ship was fully restored, there was even less to do and as the company were still involved in dealing with the *Centaur*, *Aragonite* and one or two small coasters, we were pretty much left alone.

Everyone had been very impressed by the satellite communications system that the Ministry of Defence had put aboard and it was decided to purchase a new one for the ship. After some negotiation with various companies, one was selected and duly installed. It had to be small enough to fit in the radio office which was already quite crowded. The only vacant space was on top of the receiver rack. Although the operating of it at this height was no problem at all, access to the inside was a problem because of its proximity to the deckhead. A small fax machine was also fitted for the reception of weather charts. Out on the bridge a small satellite navigation system was also fitted. Our idyllic existence continued and we visited the Goonhilly Earth Station and toured many of the outlying areas, swam in the sea, went sightseeing and generally enjoyed life.

Eventually, one of the Curnow directors saw me on board and asked what I was doing, why was I not on leave. I simply said that I had agreed with Neil to remain with the ship while his parents were in the country. After checking, he found that they had just returned to New Zealand and I was sent home on leave on the 12th July, 1983.

I remained at home for just over two months and although I had lots of leave still owing, I asked if I might rejoin the ship for the first voyage after our restoration. This was granted and I rejoined at Avonmouth on the 21st September. By this time, the *Centaur* was completing her last Curnow voyage before being returned to Straits Shipping. I was very pleased about this, although the pursers who were sailing in the *Centaur* were very disappointed that she had not been purchased to replace the ageing *St Helena*. Because most of the people wanting to travel had already gone out on the *Centaur*, we sailed from Avonmouth with only twelve passengers aboard, although we did fill up along the way.

Captain Bob Wyatt had gone on leave to be replaced by Martin Smith as captain. Quite a few of us who had been with the *St Helena* throughout the MOD charter were also back. If I harboured thoughts that things may have remained as before the Falklands, I was very much mistaken. We had entered a new era and as far as I was concerned, times had changed and the new technology we had now acquired was to alter my working life completely.

It was not that any of the equipment was difficult to operate. On the contrary, it was exceedingly simple and that is what caused the problem. In the days that ship to shore communication was made mainly in Morse code, it was often difficult and certainly expensive. Sometimes hours were spent calling the shore station before an answer was received. Then a turn number was allocated and a wait, sometimes of an hour or more was quite common. Messages were charged by the word and could turn out to be very expensive if they were more than a dozen words in length. The teleprinter which had been installed in the ship in 1979 made things a lot easier and the messages were charged according to the length of time they took to transmit. Initially, the charge was fifty pence per minute and quite a lot could be sent in that time. It was still not an automatic service, however. Long delays could be experienced while waiting for a free channel. Consequently, messages to and from the different departments both on the ship and in the office tended to be saved up and sent as a single long message. With the satellite, however, there were no delays. One simply dialled a number and pressed a button and off went the message. It was the same sort of thing with satellite telephone calls. Press a button to request the satellite and then simply dial the number. It was, of course, quite expensive, a telephone call cost about six pounds sterling per minute! The ease of the whole operation soon served to double and then treble the amount of messages which were going back and forth. As soon as those working in the office realised that they could send messages direct, they ceased to send them all in one long one once or twice a day. Instead, they sent them as and when they liked. Their arrival on the ship was not limited to when I was in the radio office. Whether I was there or not, the messages came in automatically and waited in the equipment's electronic memory until I printed them out. I had an alarm fitted in my cabin which signalled the arrival of a message. This alarm tended to sound every half-hour or so from 0800 in the morning until maybe 1900 in the evening. Many of the messages were only a few words. Although the printing and delivery of these messages did not involve much work on my part, they certainly broke up my off-duty periods. Before long, it was only at weekends that I could expect to be undisturbed during my off-duty hours. This did not only affect me, but the captain also, as it was normally he that distributed them to the various heads of department. Until we got satellite communications, the radio office was closed in port, thus allowing me to catch up with any paperwork or maintenance. The use of satellite, however, was permitted and so the ever-increasing communication workload continued unabated.

When we arrived at St Helena immediately after our restoration, I discovered that the island was advertising a free shore to ship telephone service while we were at anchor. Although this was not compulsory on my part, living next to the radio office, I could hardly help hearing them calling us on the VHF short-range radiotelephone. I felt that I could not, in all conscience, ignore such calls in case they were urgent. Although this free service was not generally abused at *St Helena*, the calls continued to trickle in and out all day and often well into the evening. At Ascension, the free calls began at 0800 in the morning and continued unabated all day until the radio station closed at 1900 or the ship sailed. Here, I found that it was even difficult to get an hour off for lunch. I initially said that I was closing down between 1230 and 1330 for lunch. The radio station accepted this without argument. Hardly had I settled down for a can of beer in my cabin, but someone came up asking for a telephone call. When I said that I was closed for lunch for an hour, I was told 'That is why I came up now, I knew you wouldn't be busy'! Thinking that it was just one call, I put it through only to be told by the shore station that they had half a dozen more calls for me. And so it went on.

This sort of thing was especially annoying when I was trying to deal with radar repairs which came up from time to time. Captain Wyatt was especially helpful in this regard. All the captains had restricted radio operator's certificates which allowed them to operate the equipment. If I was tied up with the radar, he would go in the radio office and make all the telephone calls for me until it was working again.

Despite all this, I realised that I was still better off than I would have been in any other company. I was well paid, enjoyed an excellent amount of leave and was generally quite content. I could, however, see that it was all the beginning of the end for radio officers. Before the Falklands, I was performing a skilled job which not only included the frequent use of Morse code, but also the fault diagnosis and repair of all communications equipment, radar installations, navigational equipment, the public address system and on-board telephone exchange. With the satellite equipment, although it increased the operating load, it was so simple to use that anyone could do it. At the same time, international organisations were pressing for 'satcoms', as they were called, to be fitted on ships on an international scale, thus dispensing with the need for a radio officer. Servicing of the equipment by on-board personnel was frowned on. When I asked a shore service agent what was the procedure to be followed in the event of a breakdown, I was given the arrogant answer 'We will supply a new printed circuit board to replace the faulty one for a nominal charge.' 'What is a nominal charge?' I asked. The technician replied 'Two thousand pounds or so!' When I displayed my shock, he waved it aside with a laugh and said 'A mere bagatelle to a shipping company!' Between 1979 and 1982, Neil and I had dealt with over 90 per cent of the repairs ourselves, the only cost to the company being for replacement components. It became very obvious to me, at least, that the removal of the radio officer would not necessarily mean a saving of money in the end. In 1983, plans were on the table to dispense with radio officers on an international scale by 1990. In 1983, I was 39 years old, and I realised that I had about seven years to lay plans for my future employment after 1990.

Despite the gathering clouds, life was still good and I was glad that the ship was back in normal operation again. It was on this voyage that I came across my final living link with the last commercial square-rigged sailing ships. In my early years at sea, I often sailed with older crew members who had served in square riggers. As the years passed, they all retired, but I still continued to meet them amongst the older passengers from time to time.

On this particular voyage, we had on board Commander Fryer, RN Rtd. In the late 1930s, the Admiralty decided to have a non-magnetic brigantine built for survey work. The vessel was to be called *Research*. The brigantine rig was two masts, with square sails on the foremast and a spanker and gaff topsail on the mainmast. Commander Fryer was assigned as captain designate. The biggest problem was that he had never served in sail. The Admiralty therefore paid for him to sail out to Australia on one of the Finnish grain ships and return on another one. In this way, he would be able to gain valuable experience in handling square rig. The two ships he sailed in were the big four-masted barques *Pommern* and *L'Avenir* belonging to Captain Gustaf Erikson, of Marieheim, Finland.

The *Pommern* had been built at Hamburg in 1903 for the famous German sailing ship company of Laeisz. She was 2,423 gross tons, had a length of 302 feet and a breadth of 43.2 feet. She was built at a time when sailing ships were having a hard time competing with steamers and consequently was fitted with a number of labour-saving devices and features. The uppermost square sails on the three square-rigged masts were the upper t'gallants. On a conventional sailing ship, there would be royals and maybe even skysails above these. To compensate for the loss of sail area, the remaining five square sails were far broader than normal. This tended to give ships so rigged a stumpy look. The rig was often referred to as a stump t'gallant rig. The three square-rigged masts were all identical and each yard and section interchangeable with the other masts. This made for savings on maintenance or replacement of damaged items. Halliard and brace winches were also fitted. These enabled the massive steel yards to be hoisted and swung to the required angle by a minimum number of seamen.

Commander Fryer had some excellent photographs taken on board during a storm showing the lower and upper t'gallants in ribbons shortly after they were blown out of the bolt-ropes. He also described the noise every time the ship was put over onto another tack. As the ship's bows came across the wind, the jibs

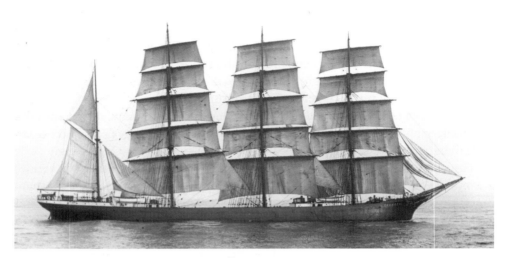

Pommern
(courtesy of J. and M. Clarkson)

L'Avenir
(courtesy of J. and M. Clarkson)

and staysails would flog and crackle like thunder until they filled on the other tack. The square sails behaved in a similar manner, but because they were far larger than the jibs the noise would be even greater, and even the hull itself would come up with a shuddering jerk as the square sails filled again. These big sailing ships of the Erikson grain fleet sailed out from Europe in ballast and loaded grain in Australia and came back to Europe around Cape Horn. Captain Erikson was a great enthusiast of sail and as long as they made a small profit, he was content. The ships were invariably secondhand and he bought them quite cheaply as commercial sail was in a definite decline after the Great War.

The other sailing ship which Commander Fryer was sent to was the *L'Avenir*, a magnificent four-masted barque which had begun life as a Belgian cargo-carrying training ship. Unlike the *Pommern*, she carried a more conventional rig which included royals above the t'gallants. She also had a very long poop deck which extended forward of the mainmast. This meant that the ship's main steering was done from almost amidships rather than right aft as in the *Pommern* which had the conventional short poop deck aft. The exposed wheel of the *Pommern* meant that in following seas, she became vulnerable to being 'pooped'. This meant a following sea breaking over the poop deck. If this happened and the helmsman was washed from the wheel, the ship could go out of control, broach to and roll over. Many a fine sailing ship has been lost in this manner.

The *L'Avenir* was sold out of the Erikson fleet shortly before World War II. She became the German cargo-carrying cadet ship *Admiral Karpfanger*. In 1938, the *Admiral Karpfanger* sailed out to Australia in 107 days. With a total complement of 60, which included 40 cadets, she sailed from Port Germein on February 8th, 1938, in company with the three-masted barque *Killoran* and the four-masted barque *Pommern*. She radioed her position to Hamburg when three weeks out from Port Germein. Eleven days later, she acknowledged a radio message and then sailed on into oblivion. She was never seen again. The four-masted barque *Viking* which sailed shortly afterwards sighted icebergs off the Horn, so it is a possibility that she may have struck one of them. After a long search for the missing ship, wreckage from the *L'Avenir* was found on Navarino Island, near the Horn, but nothing to indicate what had befallen the ship.

Commander Fryer's prospective ship, the *Research* was not actually completed until the outbreak of World War II. Her first voyage was to have been about eighteen months' duration sailing between the remote island of Tristan da Cunha and Cape Town. A cruise of three years in the Indian Ocean was then planned. All this was cancelled due to the outbreak of war. When hostilities ceased, technology had overtaken the *Research*. The tasks that she had been built to undertake were all accomplished more quickly and easily by small aircraft. The *Research* never went to sea. She lay in the River Dart throughout the war with

Heavy weather aboard a square-rigged sailing ship

only her lower masts stepped. Shortly after she was broken up, thus ending Commander Fryer's chance of a command in square-rig.

During the course of the voyage, I completed five illustrated lectures for the passengers. Two of these were my standard slide shows covering the transition from sail to steam in the Merchant Navy. The other three were by popular request about our activities in the Falklands during the MOD charter. One was completed on the outward voyage, one in Cape Town and another one on the way back home.

The Cape Town show caused me particular annoyance. It was decided that a cocktail party would be held in the main lounge for agents, VIPs and other officials. The captain and senior officers would act as hosts. On completion, they would all go down to dinner in the saloon and after coffee and liqueurs, would return to the main lounge at about 2115 hours for the slide show. Why I was not included in the cocktail party or dinner I have no idea, unless it was because I did not normally have a passenger table in the saloon. Normally, we all had to attend such things whether we liked it or not! On this occasion, I had to take an early dinner and then hang around until 2115 when they all came up for the slide show. It later transpired that Dave Roberts, the chief officer, had decided that he was not going to attend the function at all and had gone ashore with his wife and children who were travelling at the time. This left an empty space which needed to be filled, and I was told to get myself down to the lounge where the cocktail party was just starting and then take Dave Roberts's place in the saloon. I had already eaten well and had a few glasses of wine, followed afterwards by coffee and liqueurs. I was in no frame of mind to go to a cocktail party, eat another dinner, drink more wine and liqueurs and then put on a slide show. Initially I refused, and although I would not have left them in the lurch began to suggest that as the talk was voluntary I might well not do it! I got through the cocktail party by drinking 'whisky and ginger' which, by prior arrangement with Maureen and Glenda, was actually ginger on its own. Dinner was rather more difficult. I did not fare so well with the wine feeling more or less obliged to match my table companions drink for drink. The same went for the liqueurs. When the slide show finally started at about 2130, I was more than a little 'merry'. Fortunately, it went off without a hitch despite my semi-inebriated state.

This was the second Falklands talk I had given and one thing was becoming quite apparent. A number of the ship's company that did not go south with the ship seemed to take a great delight in pointing out that 'The war was over before they got there, they didn't actually do anything!' On the way home, two more talks were scheduled. The first of these also provoked a similar response. In view of this, I suggested that Captain Smith made the second one to see if it made any difference. He was glad to oblige, but again an undercurrent of subdued resentment on the part of a small minority made itself known. A highly polished brass plaque commemorating our year's service in the Falklands had been presented to the ship by the Ministry of Defence and fixed to the bulkhead in the alcove of the forward lounge. It did not take long for some unknown person to try and rip it off. Although they failed in this, it caused a bad crease across the brass. In view of this, I decided not to show further slides on the subject and revert to my 'transition from sail to steam' lectures which were always well-received by the passengers.

Several voyages later, HRH Princess Margaret visited the ship as part of the 150th Anniversary celebration of St Helena being a Crown Colony. The Princess had actually named the ship *St Helena* several years previously when it arrived from Canada at the start of the Curnow Shipping management contract. I was due to return to the ship about the time of the visit, but because of security, I got an extra two days' leave and Neil had the honour of meeting the Princess.

In 1983, the company chartered in a 12,000 gross ton passenger ship called the *World Renaissance* to make a series of cruises from Plymouth to the Cape Verde Islands, St Helena and Cape Town. These were to start on 25th November 1983 and end in Plymouth on the 23rd November the following year. By this time, the *Centaur* had completed her temporary charter and departed for the East again. The only Curnow staff member to sail on the *World Renaissance* was John Dimmock, the purser who had been with us on a temporary basis during our trooping/store ship days in the South Atlantic. We met up with the ship in St Helena, but did not go aboard as one of us was about to sail. We all looked forward to the success of this venture in the hope that the ship would be purchased and Curnow staff appointed to it in due course. This was not to be. In no time at all it became obvious that it was not a success and the big ship departed from the Curnow shipping scene.

About this time, Curnow decided to allow any of the sea staff to purchase shares in the company. In 1979 I would have jumped at the chance, but times had since changed. The investment that I had made when I was turned down for Curnow shares in 1979 was doing extremely well and in view of the very alarming decline in the British Merchant Fleet as a whole, I decided to keep out of shipping!

At the start of Voyage 35, the ship was affected by a national dock strike at Avonmouth. The officers and crew loaded the Royal Mail themselves at midnight. I was not aboard on that particular voyage, but watched the proceeding on the national news. When the ship returned, the strike was still on, so they docked at Falmouth instead of the usual Avonmouth.

Both Captain Smith and Captain Wyatt were otherwise employed on other ships at the time, so it was necessary to promote Chief Officer Mike Underwood to captain for the voyage. A new captain is always an unknown quantity even if one has got on well with them before they reached that rank. I needn't have worried, however. We had always got on well in the past, but once he received promotion we got on even better. Radio communications had by then grown to quite substantial proportions and as every message to or from the ship went through my hands, my knowledge of the company affairs was quite considerable. We had a long talk in his cabin one afternoon as soon as we were clear of the UK. We went through all the standard messages which he would be expected to send during the trip and he took in all my suggestions for the smooth running of communications. He then told me that with all he had to think about he might sometimes forget to invite me to special social occasions which all the captains held from time to time in their cabin. But I was welcome anyway. If I found out that something was going on, I could assume that I was invited regardless of whether he had mentioned it or not. Some of the officers found that he had become rather aloof, but I never found that to be the case and was glad of his support later in the voyage when we were all going through the most traumatic of experiences.

Most of the voyage passed off without incident, but all that was to change on Halloween Night, 1984. We had just passed Dakar, West Africa, in beautifully calm weather and were looking forward to arriving at Tenerife in a couple of days or so and the UK four days after that. The Halloween celebrations commenced at 2115 in the evening as soon as we had finished dinner. Most of the passengers and off-duty officers assembled in the forward lounge where frog racing was to be held. This was to be followed by a Halloween theme fancy dress parade. I remained until the frog racing had finished and went off to bed at about 2200 hours, dropping off to sleep immediately.

I was suddenly awakened by the alarm bells ringing. Before I even turned on my light, I could smell burning. The cabin had a faint haze of smoke in it. I leapt out of bed, put on trousers and jacket and went into the radio office. As I got there, the public address system burst into life with the 3rd officer calling the fire attack party, the ship's surgeon and medical party to muster im-mediately at the door to the engine room.

Once in the radio office, I checked that the satellite was on station and also switched on the main transmitter. I could hear a lot of shouting, banging and running feet outside. The lights dimmed and went out for a few seconds and then came back on again. Looking out of the window, I could see thick smoke pouring from the funnel casings and swirling up into the darkness. With the main and emergency transmitters switched on and tuned in, I was all ready to send out a call for assistance. Cadet John Harrison appeared, giving me the ship's position on a piece of paper. A few minutes later, Captain Underwood came in and told me to send out a distress message to the effect that we had a serious engine room fire and were preparing to abandon ship. Outside the radio room window, the smoke had become so thick that I could no longer see number two lifeboat which was in its davits only a few feet away. Again the lights went out and I subsequently learned that the emergency generator had choked on all the smoke. The only option left to me was to send the distress call out using the emergency transmitter which was powered by twenty-four volt batteries situated on top of the bridge. The alarm signal consisted of twelve four-second dashes, each separated by one second. This would set off auto alarm systems in other ships in the vicinity. Although twelve dashes should be sent, time permitting, only three were necessary to actuate auto alarm bells. As the fourth dash was sent out, I heard the sounds of another transmitter tuning during the one second interval between the fourth and fifth dashes. Nevertheless, I sent all twelve and followed it by the distress call giving our name and call sign. I then had to wait two minutes to give radio officers on answering ships time to get to their radio rooms in order to take down the distress message. When the two minutes were up, I again repeated the SOS signal followed by our call sign, name, position and nature of the distress, adding for good measure that we were a passenger vessel. Immediately I completed it, an answering call came in loud and clear from the *Overseas Argonaut*. He confirmed that they were less than thirty miles away and were already proceeding at maximum speed. I thanked him and then answered the American ship *Kittanning* who had also altered course towards us. The air waves were pandemonium with ships acknowledging and offering help. All the time I was communicating with the other ships, I was aware of people coming in, grabbing various items and rushing out again. Geoff, the purser, grabbed my toolbox and emptied the whole lot out on the deck before rushing off with the empty box. I later learned that he required it to take the contents of the safe with him when the ship was abandoned. Others required various tools which were quite easy to find as they were scattered about the deck! Outside I could hear a lot of clattering and banging, accompanied by a lot of shouting as the boats were prepared for lowering. The air then became so thick that I was forced to open the window. The smoke began to pour out, but I was forced at one stage to kneel on top of the teleprinter mounted on the desk below the window. As I did so, there was a loud cracking noise as I knelt on the equipment, but I was not too concerned about it at the time!

Shortly afterwards the smoke began to clear and it was with great relief that I was able to report to Captain Underwood that two ships were on their way, the nearest, being only twenty-five miles distant. By this time, the engine room had been flooded with CO_2 gas in an attempt to extinguish the flames. We had also taken on a slight list owing to the water from the fire hoses which had been used to cool the engine room casing in order to contain the fire.

The boats and life rafts were lowered to the embarkation deck and were already filled with passengers and crew members. As well as Captain Underwood, Chief Engineer Bryan Gillott, Chief Officer Bill Hughes and Electrical Officer Dave Webster had remained on the bridge. Dave had successfully restarted the emergency generator and all our lights were blazing once again. I returned to the radio office where I found that the satellite equipment, although on, was no longer useable as the dish had been turned away from the satellite because the gyro compass had become unstable due to intermittent power. So much for modern technology, I thought as I filled in the log. Although the situation remained grave, the smoke had virtually ceased pouring out of the funnel casing. Eventually, I joined the group on the bridge to report the progress of the *Overseas Argonaut*. The captain was looking down at the passengers in the swung out boat as I brought him up to date with the situation. One of them shouted up 'Are they here yet?' The captain gave a thumbs up sign and said 'Any time now!' Hardly had he finished, when there was a distant whoosh and bang as a brilliant flare soared into the night sky several miles off our port bow. As we watched it float down, we saw, far below it, the faint light of the *Overseas Argonaut*. A massive cheer went up from the boats at the welcome sight of the big tanker and the tension began to ease.

After the arrival of the tanker, all was quiet aboard the *St Helena*. The fire, although contained, continued to burn in the engine room. The panelling in both fore and aft alleyways on our two passenger decks had been hacked away with axes exposing the steel of the engine casing. The fire hoses were played on the steel from time to time to cool it down, but within half an hour of each hosing, it inevitably began to heat up again. It was decided to keep everyone aboard for the time, but keep a close watch on the bulkheads. The passengers and crew who were not immediately required were told to get some sleep on the boat deck using the camp beds normally used for deck passengers. With the failure of the air-conditioning, the normal heat of the doldrums, plus the heat radiating from the engine room, it was an extremely uncomfortable night. The captain remained awake and on the bridge throughout, but insisted that I return to my cabin behind the bridge in order to try and get some sleep. This, I found to be impossible, so I just lay on my bunk, ready for an immediate call if required.

The following day dawned hot and sticky, with the reassuring form of the giant tanker standing by at a safe distance. At last, the bulkheads began to cool down and we became more confident that the fire was at last dying down. By this time, I had the satellite communication system working again and we had communicated our plight to head office with the request for a salvage tug.

The next few days were uncomfortable for all on board, but they were extremely interesting. Although passengers are notorious for complaining about things on a smoothly running ship, we had no such problems on the disabled *St Helena*. Everyone pitched in and assisted where they could, even the most elderly. Close by, lying still and placid on a pale blue sea was the 138,000 deadweight ton tanker *Overseas Argonaut*, ready and willing to stand by as long as we required them. The close proximity of this giant was a source of great comfort to all on board.

Still listing from the amount of water from the fire hoses, the *St Helena* lay sweltering on a mirror-like sea, the whine of the emergency generator being the only sound. During the emergency, no one had suffered any serious injury. Peter Wood, the engineer who had been on watch at the time had suffered burns to his hands, but they were not serious. Bob Bendall, the 3rd engineer had got a nail stuck in the palm of his hand while he was involved in firefighting where the panelling had been hacked away, but again, it was not serious.

The equipment in the radio office, apart from the short wave teleprinter was fully functional on the emergency power. The teleprinter, however, had received serious physical damage when I knelt on top of it in my quest for fresh air. I was not overly concerned over this as I could still communicate using the satellite teleprinter, Morse code or radiotelephone. Captain Underwood put a block on all private communications in the immediate aftermath of the fire. This allowed me to keep in contact with the German salvage tug *Fairplay IX* which was steaming out to collect us. Regular contact with head office was maintained and I was also able to get the damaged teleprinter working after a fashion, although it was making a lot of spelling mistakes and over-typing some text. Despite this, it was invaluable when communicating with the tug.

After three days, the fire in the engine room seemed to have died away and the casing cooled down. Clad in breathing apparatus, 2nd engineer Tim Walpole descended to investigate the damage. It appeared that the fire had been confined to an area around the generators and although a considerable amount of damage, especially to the electrical cables, had been done, it was not a complete disaster. The main engine appeared undamaged and also the generators and main switchboard had survived.

As soon as it was confirmed that the fire was well and truly out, we advised the *Overseas Argonaut* that it was no longer necessary for them to stand by us. We offered sincere and grateful thanks for their assistance and gave them three cheers as they started their engines and slowly came round to their course and steamed off into the distance. It would be several days before the tug arrived, so we just sat it out, alone and disabled, on an empty sea.

The crew accommodation had been flooded and was in a terrible mess. Most of them slept on deck in the oppressive heat. Meals were cooked on open fires on the foredeck barbeque style. For fuel, the catering staff used the wood panelling which had been chopped out of the accommodation. Passengers, officers and crew all ate the evening meal together in the passenger dining saloon. On deck, bucket chains were formed to carry fresh water from the tanks after the lids had been unbolted. A large number of passengers volunteered to assist in this duty. Awnings were rigged to catch rainwater during the many tropical downpours that assailed us from time to time. Although the canvas appeared to be clean, the rainwater collected was absolutely filthy (global pollution?). Another large awning was rigged on the foredeck to provide some shade for the crew or anyone else who wished to escape from the discomfort of the accommodation. To add to our troubles, a large number of cricket-like insects descended on us the morning after the fire. One of our cadets, Rodney Young, had tried sleeping on top of the bridge and woke up covered from head to foot in the obnoxious insects!

When the *Fairplay IX* finally arrived, her chief mate, a huge fair-haired German, came aboard. Dressed in shorts, vest and working boots, he was polite and efficient. His first enquiry was to ask if they could provide anything for the safety and comfort of all on board? He then set about organising the tow with our chief officer and bosun. In no time at all, they returned to the tug and her powerful engines began to churn the water. As she moved off someone hoisted a huge sign at their stern with the words 'Follow me' written on it in large letters.

Who says the Germans have no sense of humour? They had taken longer to reach us than expected simply because they were towing another small vessel. When we were all moving, it was in a 'V' formation with us to port and the other vessel to starboard behind the tug.

The weather remained sweltering hot, but there was plenty to occupy ourselves with. On the first morning of the tow, I had been up very early and was helping out in the engine room. As 0800 approached, I left to go on watch. As I mounted the bridge stairs at about 0750, I could hear the satellite telephone ringing. Just as I reached it, it stopped. The officer of the watch said it had been ringing for ages, but for some reason, he had not answered it. Shortly afterwards, a message was received from the office demanding to know why I hadn't answered the telephone! Naturally, I was extremely annoyed about this as I had been down below in my off-duty time helping the hard-pressed electrical officer. Captain Underwood was none too pleased about the tone of the message either, but said that we would keep a low profile on this one until the time was right. In the meantime, he said, the engine room would just have to do without my help! This actually made things a lot easier as it meant that when I was off duty, I was off duty and only required to answer the auto alarm or the satellite telephone if it rang.

After an uneventful, but hot and sweaty few days, we arrived in the Port of Dakar, West Africa. We were docked in the Dakar Marine shipyard for repairs to be assessed. A large proportion of the passengers volunteered to remain with the ship, but this was impossible and they were all flown home.

The repair took several weeks with a heavy workload for all onboard. Our lifestyle changed dramatically. All the crew moved into the empty passenger accommodation. We all breakfasted together in the dining saloon. Midday meals were also communal cold-buffet style on the promenade and poop decks. In the evening, when work was over for the day, officers and crew socialised together in the forward passenger lounge.

Officer reliefs began almost immediately. Before the voyage had started, my opposite number, Neil, had asked if we could change voyages in order for him to spend Christmas at home. This would have involved me doing one and a half voyages and flying home from Cape Town. He would then fly out to Cape Town to rejoin for the next one and a half voyages. I was not too keen on this idea. Not because I was bothered about spending Christmas on the ship or to be awkward. The fact was I disliked the discomforts of flying, especially long hauls such as UK to Cape Town. Once we were in Dakar, however, things changed. We were told that after repairs were completed, we would not sail north, but go south to Cape Town again via Ascension and St Helena. With this in mind, I sent a message to Neil saying that if he still wanted Christmas at home, I would remain for the repair and complete the voyage to Cape Town and back to the UK. This would give him Christmas at home. At the same time, it would amount to me doing two continuous voyages. Consequently, when he came back, it would also be for two consecutive voyages! He quickly agreed to this, so we both got what we wanted.

The workload during the repair was exceptional and for several weeks I was confined to the radio office and bridge with fifteen minutes or so off for meals. Although the use of conventional communications was not permitted while in port, satellite communications were and these continued on a more or less continual stream from sun-up until well into the evening. As time went by, communications lessened and the company enquired as to how all the officers were filling their time. When it came to me, Captain Underwood pointed out that I was not helping in the engine room any longer, because I had been confined to the radio office on their orders for practically twenty-four hours a day! They then relented and said that now the pressure was off, they had no objections to me working elsewhere in the ship, if necessary!

Despite expressing a wish to remain and see the ship back to the UK, the captain was relieved by Captain Bob Wyatt, a good friend of long standing. At the weekends, we would usually take ourselves off to a local hotel in company with Dr. Stevenson, ship's surgeon, his wife Betty and the two stewardesses, Maureen and Glenda. We usually spent the whole afternoon lazing by the hotel swimming pool and going in it from time to time in order to cool off.

Two days before we were due to sail, the satellite alarm went off in the middle of the night. Looking in the top, I could see wisps of smoke rising from a one-inch flame which was licking up one of the printed circuit boards. A quick puff extinguished it as I switched the whole thing off. It had finally succumbed to excessive use in the tropical climate. Had it been any other piece of equipment, I would have stood a good chance of repairing it using my own resources. In this case it was impossible. The damaged printed circuit board was a mass of integrated circuits and one of these had been completely destroyed. We carried no spares as repairs to boards were considered 'neither practical nor possible'! The local communications specialists had no spare boards either, which was not surprising. Weeks earlier, the Dakar service engineers had failed to repair the short wave teleprinter saying that as it was an electromechanical device, it was obsolete! In any case, the use of normal medium- or short-wave transmitters was prohibited in port, so we were without direct contact with the outside world.

On communicating with head office via the agent, we were told that once we were out at sea again, it was essential that full communications were maintained, even if it meant the radio officer (me) sitting in the radio office sending Morse for twenty-four hours a day! All this was no doubt said in the heat of the moment as in normal times relations with head office were very friendly indeed. After the trauma of the ship almost being lost, plus the stress of working long hours in the most uncomfortable conditions, this statement only served to 'get my back up'! I had used Morse code every single day that I had spent at sea in the past twenty-three years, however, and I estimated that I could manage at least 1,500 words per hour and if I only spent four hours a day at it, the result would still be in excess of 6,000 words. At a cost of about 60 pence per word the communication bill would be in excess of £2,400 per day! The thought initially gave me great satisfaction. The following morning, however, I had calmed down, and with no communications to deal with until we were at sea again, I took out the damaged teleprinter and stripped it down. I spent hours fiddling with the strained and damaged mechanisms and shortly before sailing time, I succeeded in getting it to function almost perfectly. Only the odd letter was over-typed and would cause no problem.

When we sailed, it was a pleasure to get out of the heat and onto the relative cool of the ocean once again. Apart from the air-conditioning not working and the damage to the alleyways and crew cabins, the ship performed as well as before. We called at Ascension and St Helena, picking up a few passengers on the understanding that the accommodation was not up to scratch yet. No one complained though, and the voyage south was pleasant enough. No comment was made of the fact that the teleprinter was working again after shore servicemen had declared it damaged beyond repair only a few weeks before! On arrival Cape Town, a new printed circuit board arrived for the satellite. Within minutes of replacing it, the satellite communications were up and running again. More repairs were effected in Cape Town and the ship was more or less back to normal when we sailed north.

The whole affair of the fire and Dakar left no traumatic mark on any of us. It was simply another interesting experience of life at sea which had been taken in our stride. If anything, we gained considerable satisfaction knowing that we had all done our duty as required and the final outcome was the ship being returned to service. It did give me cause for concern about the future though. If the ship had been lost, I would certainly have been made redundant as the company only had one ship large enough to carry a radio officer, and that was the *St Helena*.

In 1984, I was 40 years old with 23 years at sea and more than a million sea miles behind me. Trained in the days of valves, I was now surrounded by transistorised equipment on which I had never had any real training other than that of long experience. Where communication at sea had once been a highly skilled profession, it had degenerated into a very simple procedure when using the satellite. Radio officers were rapidly becoming nothing more than 'radio operators' and general electronic 'handymen', useful, but not really necessary. This had been brought home to me fairly soon after our arrival in Dakar. The company was thoughtful enough to arrange two full-day bus tours of the area, each taking half of the ship's company at a time. Captain Underwood asked me which one I wanted to go on. I pointed out that I couldn't go on either, because communications were heavy and sustained. At the same time, I was not really bothered by this, but thanked him for his concern. He then suggested that I give him a crash course in satellite communications and he would deal with it all himself when I took a break. For a full day he sat in the radio office with me and went through the various procedures. By evening, I felt that he was quite proficient at it. The following day, I went on the tour and thoroughly enjoyed the scenery and the relaxation. We toured the area, going out into the bush, crossing a river in dugout canoes, looked at giant ant hills and baobab trees. We visited an African village where we were made most welcome and not continually pestered for money which is the normal experience of the seaports. Then we spent the rest of the day lazing on a beach by a hotel complex. On returning to the ship, I found that communications had been maintained without a hitch by the captain and, as he remarked 'The office never even knew!' Ten years earlier, when Morse was king, this sort of thing would have been impossible. A sign of things to come!

On the other hand, servicing of modern equipment was often 'mission impossible' and shore service engineers would simply replace faulty printed circuit boards with new ones. Servicing skills were still required for other areas such as conventional radio equipment, radar, public address systems, crew videos, television sets, photocopiers, bridge electronics etc. I was also expected to help out with the sophisticated electronics that were creeping into engine rooms throughout ships in general. Plus the numerous bits and pieces that the passengers would send up for repair. Because of these extra duties, I felt that at the moment my position was secure. But the ship was 21 years old and at that time we did not know if the British government would see fit to replace it when it was worn out. In the normal course of events, we could expect it to carry on until its 30-year survey which was due in 1993. If by any reason it was not replaced, I would have found myself redundant at the age of 49 with no prospects of obtaining another position at sea. It was also difficult to imagine what I could do ashore with my outdated qualifications. As a result, I began to make plans for the future—something I had never done before!

On my return to the UK I was delighted to hear that I was to have four months leave. In the past, I had enjoyed article writing for various magazines. I had been quite successful at it and had even written a small book on ship-modelling which had sold well. I had given it up in the late 1970s because I became tired of the constant typing, re-typing and correcting of manuscripts, to say nothing of messing about with carbon paper. Early in my leave, I purchased my first computer word-processor. Despite what the publicity material said , I found this exasperating device was completely 'user hostile'! Taking a two-week course gave me a lot of clues and I eventually mastered it. I could write again! I was pleased to find that my articles were accepted with the regularity of previous years, but the time between acceptance and publication had lengthened to between one and four years. Once this became apparent, I again dropped the idea of becoming a writer, but continued to develop computer skills as they were obviously going to be part of the future whether we liked it or not! Another big change in my lifestyle came about during my two voyages off. I met Christine, whom I was to marry less than two years later.

From time to time over the past two decades, especially when undergoing stressful passages such as rough weather, heavy workloads etc. I had pondered over the idea of packing up the sea and remaining at home. As is usual with sailors, however, as soon as the immediate crisis had passed and things settled down again, I once again fell into a contented routine and abandoned any thoughts of leaving. Generally, I was supremely happy at sea. I had so far weathered all the changes very well. Although I had thought that life could not be better than the one I had enjoyed in the Union-Castle liners, I found it even better in the *St Helena*. For every two months at sea, I got two months leave. The pay was very good and conditions onboard were comfortable despite the diminutive size of the ship, to say nothing of her age. I was sailing with people I had known since the mid 1960s and the company was not forever pressing me to gain more qualifications. There was no radio superintendent in the office and whatever work or decisions that were to be made pertaining to the radio and navigational equipment on the ship were made by Neil and myself.

An example of this concerned the teleprinter that I had accidentally damaged during the fire. When the ship returned to the UK immediately after the fire, the shore servicemen were called in to give it a thorough overhaul. On seeing it they had a good laugh and said it was completely obsolete and no spares were available. The company therefore decided to purchase a new system with a VDU monitor and word-processor in place of the old electromechanical system. When the new system was fitted, I asked the shore servicemen if they would allow us anything on the old one. They had another good laugh and said 'We give these museum pieces away when they come in!' An idea immediately sprang to my mind and I asked if they had another identical one that they wanted to give away. They promised to have a look in their office. True to their word, they arrived the following day with an identical teleprinter 'free and for nothing'. During the course of the voyage, I eventually brought our old machine up to

100% again by taking pieces from the scrap one which had been given to me in Avonmouth. On our return, I contacted the company and said that if they would purchase a control unit for it, I would install it on the company tanker *Bosun Bird*. They agreed to this and the control unit was put aboard immediately prior to my next voyage. On arrival at St Helena, I had the control unit and teleprinter sent across and then spent the next few days on board the *Bosun Bird* figuring out how to connect it all up. Eventually, I got the system working and the following voyage, Neil completed the installation by tidying it all up and making a permanent fitting of it. Every day, while we were at sea, we had daily schedules with the captain of the *Bosun Bird*. As the small ship had no radio officer, these were conducted on the short-wave radiotelephone. I always found these hard going as there was often interference and the signals were very faint at long distance. My plan was to render the telephone schedules obsolete and communicate by the teleprinter keyboards. The tests proved successful as the teleprinter was able to ignore interference and weak signals to a great extent. Unfortunately, Captain Dodkins did not really like the idea and insisted on keeping up with the telephone schedule, preferring what he called 'the personal touch'. So in the end, we were really no better off in terms of time saved. Eventually, however, the company started sending telex messages direct to the *Bosun Bird* rather than sending them to us on telex with instructions to 'Pass to *Bosun Bird*'. The continued trouble-free operation of our old teleprinter gave me a lot of satisfaction when I recalled how the 'experts' had said that it was beyond repair!

This sort of thing would never have happened in a large company where we were simply told what to do. The old printer would simply have been scrapped and that would have been the end of the matter! Involvement in company decisions which we all enjoyed with Curnow tended to make for a happier relationship between office and sea staff. During my leave, I soon forgot the discontent that was brewing in me towards the end of our stay in Dakar, but at the same time I realised that times were changing at an ever increasing speed as far as radio officers were concerned and I only had a few years at most to do something about it! I regarded the fire and Dakar as a 'wake up' call!

In 1986, the ship was scheduled for a trial call at the remote island of Tristan da Cunha which lay about 36 degrees south and 12 degrees west. If the call was successful, it was planned to make one visit per year from then on. I was rather disappointed not to be aboard during the first call at this remote spot. During the voyage, they encountered very bad weather while close to the island and also on the way across to Cape Town after the call. The ship experienced the heaviest roll of her career to that date—namely 37 degrees one way and 32 degrees the other way!

The following year, Christine and I were married and she accompanied me for the voyage a few weeks afterwards. Unfortunately, we had bad weather almost every day, even in the tropics which was most unusual. The Cape Town call was cut short for some reason, so I had little chance to show her around the city. After a voyage off as usual, we both rejoined for an almost normal voyage. But after leaving St Helena southbound, the ship began to leak through the propeller shaft bearing. This was not dangerous as the pumps could easily cope and the ingress of water was not excessive. It had to be fixed, however, and we were dry-docked in Cape Town after completion of cargo. Dry-docks are usually very uncomfortable experiences as bathrooms cannot be used and the shore facilities are usually poor. Also the air-conditioning was turned off and as it was the middle of summer things got quite hot onboard.

Several voyages before, the *Bosun Bird* had suffered a broken crankshaft and was found to be beyond economical repair. She was therefore sold. This resulted in Captain Paddy Dodkins becoming redundant. When we arrived in Cape Town, Paddy and his wife Mary were living in a small house at the seaside resort of Seapoint. They kindly invited anyone who wanted to visit to go along. Only Christine and I took up the offer and spent a pleasant evening with Paddy and Mary. When we returned to the ship in the taxi, Christine paid the driver and got a small amount of change. When we got back to our cabin, she declared that she thought that she had been passed a dud coin in the dark because it felt rather 'heavy'. On looking at the 'dud' I found to my astonishment (and delight) that it was a British golden sovereign. Next morning we took it to a jewellers' shop in Cape Town where the jeweller told us it was an old English shilling! Knowing exactly what an old English shilling looked like, we took it to another jeweller who offered us £20 for it. We declined and sold it in the UK for £58!

The following year it was decided to call again at Tristan da Cunha, and I found myself looking forward to visiting this remote British Colony. Shortly after leaving St Helena, I was sitting in my cabin one warm afternoon working on a ship model. Colin, the purser called in with a message. Seeing what I was doing he remarked, 'You won't be able to do that sort of thing off Tristan!' 'Why not?' I asked. He then launched into a colourful description of hurricane force winds lashing the sea into a fury. 'The South Atlantic sorts out the men from the boys!' he declared with a knowing look. I pointed out that during the MOD charter, I had spent almost a year in the South Atlantic sailing regularly to the Falklands and South Georgia. Tristan lay at about 37 South, Port Stanley 52 South, Grytviken (South Georgia) 54 South and the infamous Cape Horn 56 South. 'Tristan,' I said 'is not even in the roaring forties and over a thousand miles north in latitude from South Georgia!' He dismissed all this with a knowing look and went away. As the voyage progressed and Tristan drew closer, the weather became better and better. The day we sighted the cloud-capped island, the sea was like a mirror and the sun shone like we were in the tropics. At the anchorage there was a bit of a swell, but certainly not enough to disturb our peaceful routine aboard the little ship.

The island of Tristan da Cunha was first discovered by the Portuguese in 1506. When Napoleon Bonaparte was exiled to St Helena in 1815, Tristan da Cunha was annexed to Britain a year later. A garrison was established in order to prevent the French using it as a base from which to mount a rescue operation for their Emperor. When the garrison was no longer required, one man decided to remain. That man was Corporal William Glass, born in Kelso, Scotland in 1787. William Glass then began to recruit for companions on his lonely outpost. He was joined in 1816 by his wife Maria, from Cape Town. Males of the first generation of Tristanians were Alexander Cotton who arrived in 1821 and Thomas Swain who arrived in 1826. Both these men were English. First generation women included Sarah Jacobs of St Helena, who arrived in 1827 and Maria Williams, also of St Helena, who arrived the same year. More settlers joined the permanent residents, including a number of shipwrecked sailors. Two of these were Andrea Repetto and Gaetano Lavarello of the Italian barque *Italia*. They decided to remain after their barque was wrecked on the island in 1892. During the years I visited the island, the family surnames of the islanders consisted of Hagan, Rogers, Glass, Lavarello, Swain, Green and Repetto. In recent years, they have been joined by the name Patterson, brought by an Englishman who married a Tristanian and settled on the island.

When one considers the remoteness of Tristan, it is quite remarkable how many ships managed to get wrecked there. Between 1872 and 1953 the barquentine *Henry B. Paul* came to grief on the island. The barques *Olympia*, *Mabel Clark*, *Italia*, *Helen S. Lea* and *Glen Huntley* were wrecked there. The giant five-masted barque *Kobenhavn* disappeared in the vicinity. The full-rigged ship *Allanshaw* struck Tristan's rocks on March 23rd, 1893 while en route from Liverpool towards Calcutta with a cargo of salt. As far as I can ascertain, the last shipwreck was the yacht *Coimbra* in 1953.

In 1961, the volcano erupted next to Edinburgh, the island's only settlement. The severity of the eruption was such that a number of ships had to be diverted to take off all the inhabitants. Their way of life had changed little over the 145 years that had passed since William Glass settled there. The Tristanians found modern life in Britain intolerable, despite the welcome they received. They remained together in a close-knit circle, longing to get home. Eventually, the eruption died down and an advance party of twelve, including the headman Willie Repetto, returned to Tristan. Within a year, most of the islanders had returned home. Although the fish factory had been engulfed by the molten lava,

The settlement of Edinburgh, Tristan da Cunha

the settlement had generally survived unscathed. While the eruption was taking place, the officers and men of HMS *Leopard* carefully removed all valuables and personal belongings for safe keeping until the island became inhabitable again. Most of the livestock which had been left on the island managed to survive, despite being untended for a considerable time.

Now, there is a modern school, government offices, a small hospital and a small harbour for the boats. All the houses have running water, indoor sanitation, electricity and televison systems. During my visits, the electricity supply was turned off quite early in the evening. Consequently it was a case of 'early to bed, early to rise' for the islanders. Their main income is from fishing and the sale of postage stamps and the island is self-sufficient, not costing the British taxpayer a penny. The islanders enjoy full employment, youth clubs, sports clubs, a library and cinema shows. Crime is to all intents and purposes non-existent on the island. The hard life that they have endured since the founding of the colony in 1816 has forged a stable, contented community of which Corporal William Glass would have been proud could he see it today.

To get ashore, it was necessary to go down a vertical pilot ladder and jump into one of the cargo lighters. There were no passenger boats as such. When the boat was full, it would head off for the little harbour. Running in through the narrow entrance to the little harbour was quite exhilarating as the swells were running quite high close in to the shore. I made my first landfall with Rodney Young, our St Helenan 3rd officer. He had a penfriend on the island and first of all we called to see Marion and her husband, Albert. We then visited a number of homes including the Swains, Repettos and Lavarellos. We were made most welcome in each and the lager flowed freely at each call. We also stopped off at the school and as we were being shown around we could hear the younger children singing 'Soldier, soldier, won't you marry me with your musket fife and drum?' When we entered the classroom, they all stopped and stood up quietly as the teacher explained who we were. Despite the southern latitudes it became quite warm during the afternoon and I was sorry I had brought my raincoat along. We visited the foot of the volcano which had created havoc in 1961. Although the lava had cooled, it was still broken and dark against the lush green grass of the settlement. Clouds of steam still coiled and eddied out of the burned heap of slag even then, twenty-odd years on. It made a very interested addition to our schedule and I always looked forward to our annual visits in the years to come. Despite the purser's prophesy of extreme weather conditions, we never experienced any while I was aboard during the annual calls made between 1986 and 1992!

After I got married, I was never quite so content at sea, except when Christine accompanied me. It seemed sensible to remain at sea , if possible, until the ship's thirty-year survey which was due in 1993. It seemed unlikely that she would be allowed to carry on as a passenger ship after that date unless vast amounts of money were spent on her. In about 1986, however, the British government decided that they would place an order for a new custom-built passenger ship to replace the ageing *St Helena*. Tenders were put out to British shipyards and in due course the contract to build the new ship went to the famous yard of Hall, Russell, Aberdeen. This caused a tremendous amount of elation at Curnow Shipping, on board the ship and also on the island of St Helena.

Things tend to move rather slowly in shipbuilding circles and it was not until March 1987 that plans of the proposed new ship were presented to Curnow, the ship and the island. Eventually, the keel was laid and building work proceeded. When the hull was almost complete, Hall, Russell found themselves in the hands of the receivers and work stopped for a time. A. & P. Appledore then took over the yard and work recommenced. The final stages of the fitting out of the new ship caused considerable upheaval amongst the sea staff. With a number of the officers standing by it at Aberdeen, the rest of us remained on the old ship.

When it came time for a radio officer to go, Captain Smith told me that Neil had been chosen, because he had joined the company before me. This was a great disappointment, of course, but was only fair. I consoled myself with the fact that life in shipyards seemed to alternate between extreme boredom and frantic activity. Although I would have liked to have relieved him from time to time in the yard, this never happened and when the ship was ready to go into service, I was one of the few officers who had never even visited it!

I had been asked to build a series of models of ships which had called regularly at the island since 1814. These would be permanently displayed aboard the new ship. The models consisted of the first *St Helena*, a small schooner, the Indiaman *Blenheim*, the full-rigged passenger sailing ship *Torrens*, the Union-Castle liners *Guildford Castle* and *Kenya Castle*, and *Good Hope Castle* the old *St Helena* which had been on the run since 1978 and was about to be replaced and finally, the tanker *Bosun Bird*.

The new ship was to be named *St Helena* and in order to avoid confusion while the old ship was still running, the old ship was renamed *St Helena Island* for the last three voyages. This caused utter confusion as far as communications were concerned. Anyone wishing to send a message to the old ship rarely told the radio station that it had been renamed *St Helena Island*, so the message invariably went in the traffic lists as *St Helena*, which was now, of course, the new ship. As they were still fitting out, they were not in a position to receive traffic lists and receive the messages. Every time their call sign appeared in a traffic list, I had to call up the radio station involved and explain that the message was probably for us.

In August 1990, we returned to Falmouth instead of Avonmouth. The plan was to rendezvous there with the new ship. The new ship would then load cargo and passengers and sail off on her maiden voyage. We would remain in Falmouth until the new ship had proved herself. If, due to unforeseen circumstances, the new ship did not perform in a satisfactory manner, we would make another voyage while she was sorted out. Lying alongside in Falmouth fully manned, but with very little to do was quite a pleasant interlude which we all proceeded to make the most of. After a few days, however, the company asked me to build a model of a small ship which they were hoping to buy or charter. This would be used in tendering for a new service. I was therefore sent home to do this. The idea was gradually forming in my mind that I could become a full-time ship model builder as the models were always in demand. After two weeks, when it was almost completed, I was summoned back in a hurry. The new ship was not ready and the old one was required to sail out as far as Cape Town from where we would all be flown home and the ship sold. I rushed back to Falmouth and we sailed immediately for Avonmouth where we loaded cargo and passengers. I completed their model between Falmouth and Avonmouth. Once we were out at sea, we were told that we would not be flown home from Cape Town, but would return to Cardiff where we would rendezvous with the new ship. It was also confirmed that Cardiff was to be the permanent home port of the new vessel.

So, off we went again and completed our final voyage, number 70. During the outward voyage, the secondary radar broke down with unusual violence. There was a sharp 'crack' and smoke began to pour out of the display unit. We switched it off immediately and when I removed the cover, small flames were visible, licking up one of the printed circuit boards. This was quickly blown out. In the three or four day run to Cape Town, I was unsuccessful in effecting a repair. It was completely dead and even the scanner would not rotate. Radar engineers were called in Cape Town and after two days they declared it a 'write-off', and departed. We still had our main radar, but I did not like to be beaten. I said to Captain Wyatt, that if he authorised fifty pounds or so, I would go ashore and purchase whatever spares I considered it needed to at least get it going as far as Cardiff. He agreed, and the money was supplied by the purser. After a morning ashore, I returned with bags of resistors, capacitors and transistors. I then spent the remainder of the time in Cape Town working on it. By the time we left, I had the scanner rotating again. I also had the display and range rings back, but still no picture. It became an obsession and a point of honour to arrive in Cardiff with it working. Before we left St Helena, I finally got it working on the thirty-six-mile range, which was excellent for everyday use. It remained working until we docked at Cardiff. On arrival, it was switched off, but it never worked again!

As we entered the locks at Cardiff on 12th November, 1990, I caught my first glance of the new ship. She looked very modern and stumpy, rather like a cross-channel ferry. We berthed astern of her, back to back—what was to be the first and last meeting of the two ships. The photograph was taken by Rodney Young who was about to sail with the ship as 2nd officer on her maiden voyage. Rodney, over the course of the next eight or nine years was to rise to chief officer and eventually became the first *St Helena*n to take command of the *St Helena*.

As night fell, we were plunged into darkness. Although the lights were restored, the generator was faulty and became erratic. This gave a background sound reminiscent of an undulating wail and the lights faded from full brilliance to a dim glow and then back up to full brilliance again. This carried on for some time, giving rise to knowing whispers and furtive glances among the superstitious to the effect that 'She's dying!' In the miserable, cold weather and the knowledge that she had made her last St Helena voyage, I must confess, it did seem so! The same evening, the satellite communications failed, never to work again.

Most of us made a beeline for the new ship and wandered around in a general state of awe. At 6,500 tons gross, she was twice the size of the old ship and appeared massive. In truth, she was still very small compared with the passengers ships of 25,000 tons plus that I had sailed on a dozen or so years earlier. I was especially impressed by the spacious radio office which was the last word in modern communications. In addition to the standard equipment, there was the satellite communications, incorporating fax, telex, e-mail and radiotelephone services. There were also three separate VDU monitors in the radio office. I realised that this was the most sophisticated radio room I had ever seen. Those on the Union-Castle passenger lines paled into insignificance beside it.

Eventually, we returned to the *St Helena Island*, which now seemed small and drab with her erratic lighting. After dinner in the evening, Captain Bob Wyatt, Chief Engineer Bryan Cooper and a number of other officers congregated in my cabin and we drank and talked of the last dozen years with more than a little sadness that our small ship was at the end of her life.

A service of dedication was held aboard the new ship later on, but I did not attend.

Instead, I paced the darkened bridge of the old *St Helena* reminiscing about the past as it began to dawn on me that an era had come to an end and things would never be the same again. I signed off the following morning and went home for what I expected to be two months' leave while the new ship completed her maiden voyage.

Chapter 5

The Old Order Changeth

When I arrived home on leave, I fully expected to remain there until the new ship returned in about two months, time. My expectations were short lived. Within a week, Captain Wyatt telephoned to say that when he had switched the second radar on, prior to moving the old ship from Cardiff to Newport for dry-dock, it had failed to work and did not show any signs of life. I gave him my opinion that it was beyond economical repair and he in turn communicated this to the company. A few days later they contacted me, asking me to look round for a replacement radar and organise the fitting of it. The *St Helena Island* was to be sold to South African interests and renamed *Avalon*. Her new home port was to be Durban, South Africa, and she was to be employed cruising the Seychelles. Curnow was to maintain an interest in the ship's new employment and Bob Wyatt was to take command initially. A number of the other officers would be going along as well, but the crew were to be Zulus, recruited from Durban.

After some shopping around and negotiations with various supply firms, I chose a small radar and arranged a date for the fitting of it. I then travelled to Newport the day before in order to watch over the fitting and also brief the new radio officer on the workings of the radio department.

As I travelled down by train, the weather was atrocious. It was cold, dark and windy with moderate to heavy snow. When I arrived at the dry-dock, I was met with a scene of utter black depression. The old ship was in the throes of a refit prior to sale. I could see the sparks flying round the stern where welders

Dining room of the new St Helena
(courtesy of St Helena Line)

were at work in the vicinity of the rudder and propeller. The snow was wet and the area was churned with mud and dirty slushy snow. Picking my way aboard over various cables and pieces of staging, I arrived in the forward lounge. The heating was off and the lights were dim. In one corner there was a large heater in front of which sat Brian Cooper, chief engineer, looking more like a lumberjack than his usual smart self. He was only standing by while the ship was dry-docked. There were a few other familiar faces about, but no one seemed very happy about the situation. Being cold and hungry, I found that I had also arrived late for dinner and they had all finished apart from the 4th engineer who had also missed out. Presently, Jill Edwards, the new chef, wandered in to the lounge. She had first sailed in the ship as passenger some voyages before and had become very enamoured of sea life in general. Being in the catering trade, she had applied to the company for a job as chef, and when the vacancy for a chef in the newly named *Avalon* came up, she got it. On hearing that I had not had anything to eat, she kindly went off to the galley and made two superb chicken dinners for the 4th engineer and myself.

I located the new radio officer, whom I already knew. He had travelled as a supernumerary deck officer on the ship several years before. Because of the impending demise of the position of radio officer, he was making preparations to become a deck officer, but for the time being was to revert to his old job. We went up to the radio office and I gave him a run through all the equipment. The satellite communications, which had failed on arrival day, was still proving erratic. Although shore servicemen were called, the fault was not rectified and it remained faulty. At that time, satellite communications were not compulsory, so it would not delay the sailing in any way. I was rather annoyed to hear that someone in the office had told the radar installation engineers that there was no hurry to install the new radar, they could do it whenever convenient. Because of this, they were not arriving the following morning as I had arranged, but 'some time later'. Previous experience of installation engineers told me that this was more likely to be another 'last minute' job towards the end of the dry-dock.

I slept in a passenger cabin that night and was fairly comfortable as there were plenty of spare blankets. The following morning, the weather had deteriorated further and it was bitterly cold and windy with lots of snow and sleet about. The only cheerful faces on board seemed to be the new Zulu crew who were 'working with a will' on deck. After breakfast, I thought I would have a nostalgic tour of the docks from which I had sailed on a regular basis 28 years before. It was a depressing day for that sort of thing. As I walked along the quay, it was very overcast and the wind was blowing hard. Passing where another dry-dock had once been, I saw that it was filled up to the top with rubble. The buildings around were in ruins. I remembered walking this way in 1964 while I was serving in the ore carrier *Sagamore*, and stopping by this very dry-dock to look at the old tramp ship *Baron Inverclyde*. She was undergoing repairs after a collision in the English Channel. Everything had been bright and cheerful then, a scene of bustling nautical activity, but now it was all run down dereliction. Next I came to the iron ore quay where I had left another ore carrier, the *Joya McCance*, in 1962. When I left the *Joya McCance*, the ore quay was almost new and, despite the iron ore dust, it had a fresh look about it. The quay was still there, but it was overgrown with weed and the cranes and buildings had gone. In those days, there had been a bridge to the other side of the dock to another jetty where I had visited the *Canberra Star* in the summer of 1964. Of the bridge, there was no sign and where the *Canberra Star* once lay, the jetty had collapsed into the harbour. I persevered a little longer, but as the whole harbour system came into view, I could see no other ships and it was beginning to snow again so I returned to the *St Helena Island*.

On my return, I found that there was no sign of the radar engineers, so I decided to go home. There seemed little point in hanging about for an indefinite

111

period waiting for something to happen. The train journey home was delayed by the bad weather, but I finally arrived and put all gloomy thoughts behind me. It was, however, becoming increasingly obvious that during the years I had spent in the *St Helena*, the Merchant Navy had declined more than I had realised. Eventually, the company advised me that the new radar had been fitted and the newly named *Avalon* had departed for South Africa.

From time to time, Captain Wyatt telephoned me from South Africa with news of how things were going. The erratic behaviour of the satellite communications that defied all efforts to repair it, the satisfactory performance of the new radar and other electronic systems. It appeared that the first cruises of the *Avalon* were quite successful and interesting, but passenger numbers soon fell off and the whole project looked set for failure.

After the new ship left Tenerife on her homeward journey, I began to make ready to rejoin. For the moment, I felt rejuvenated with the prospects of joining a brand new ship and all that entailed. A few days before they were due back, however, I received a telephone call from the company saying that there had been a catastrophic engine failure and the ship had had to limp into Lisbon for temporary repairs. I was told that it would be at least ten days before she got back for repairs, which were scheduled for Falmouth.

I subsequently learned that the ship had been having trouble with the cooling system of the port engine on the way out. A similar defect then occurred in the starboard engine after leaving Tenerife on the homeward bound leg. With bad weather forecast for the Bay of Biscay, it was decided to divert to Lisbon for temporary repair. Before reaching that port, however, a connecting rod in the starboard engine broke and smashed a hole in the engine casing. This happened during the night and the noise and vibration of the breaking rods was said to be 'horrific'. The engines were immediately shut down and the damage assessed. The starboard engine was damaged beyond repair and was a write-off. They struggled into Lisbon on the port engine operating at 40% normal power. Representatives of the engine builders flew out to Lisbon and declared that a new engine would have to be fitted. In due course, the ship sailed from Lisbon and arrived in Falmouth in late January 1991.

After I joined the ship, we lay alongside for a while as preparations were made for fitting a new engine. During this time, I had very little to do. There had been a number of problems with the communications equipment in general, but these were being dealt with under the guarantee. The satellite communications had been very erratic and actually failed again as it was being demonstrated to me. Locating the problem proved troublesome initially. But with a mind 'unclouded by fact', I climbed into the large dome above the bridge to have a look round. This dome housed the dish which tracked the satellite.

After I climbed in through the hatch, I pushed the dish around and moved to the other side. As I did so, the whole dome fell sideways a couple of inches. This was very alarming as it felt like it was going to fall off the post. If it did, the whole lot, with me inside, would plunge over the bridge front and down onto the foredeck. Very gingerly, I edged back to the access hatch and climbed down onto the post. Then I inspected the holding-down nuts. They were all in place and there was actually no danger of the dome coming off the post. The trouble was, there were no washers under the nuts. The nuts had been tightened down to the end of their threads, but that left an inch of play underneath which should have been filled by washers. This allowed the dome to move about and no doubt contributed to the erratic behaviour. A couple of fitters soon rectified the problem for me and I had another look round inside. Pulling one of the multi-connection plugs out, I saw that one of the pins had been bent right over and was not engaging the socket into which it was supposed to go. This was an earthing pin and I had no great hopes of it making any difference to the performance once it was corrected. In this I was wrong, once it was straightened and fitted properly, the satellite communications gave no further trouble.

With shore service engineers coming and going at long intervals, I found life very pleasant in Falmouth. The ship was generally far more comfortable than the old one and the cabin much bigger. One disappointing fact was that I had only one window and this looked out onto the side of a bright orange lifeboat. I had no sea view like the others. The senior officers such as captain, chief engineer, chief officer and 2nd engineer all had luxurious cabins with dayroom, bedroom and bathroom. All the rest were single cabins, each with a bathroom and all more or less identical apart from the purser and purser catering who had slightly larger ones which were more comfortably fitted out.

The large radio office also contained the public address and fire alarm systems. On the old ship, the fire alarms were based on a simple electro-mechanical system and were looked after by the electrical officer. On the new ship, they came under the control of the radio officer. Consequently, I would have the added burden of testing the bells, fire detection and smoke alarms throughout the ship every voyage. The four lifeboats were modern types completely enclosed and two of them had hand-cranked lifeboat transmitters in them. There were also a number of EPIRBs about the ship ('Emergency Position Indicating Radio Beacons'). If the ship sank, they were designed to float free and transmit a distress call which could be picked up by the satellite or passing aircraft. They also came under my control. It was all the very latest and most sophisticated equipment in the Merchant Navy and it was all very daunting.

I remained on the ship in Falmouth from 24th January, 1991 until 5th March when I went home on leave without even having sailed in the ship. During this

The main lounge of the new St Helena

time, the repairs were completed and a new starboard engine fitted. Christine and I then joined the ship in Cardiff on the 8th April, 1991 for our first voyage in the new *St Helena*. Before sailing, we had time to have a good look round Cardiff which was to be our home port from now on. I had sailed from there in my younger days in the *Sagamore*, but it was all changed and I found it difficult to recognise the dock where we had once discharged iron ore in the early 1960s. On completion of cargo and embarkation of passengers, we sailed during the first week in April, 1991. As soon as we were out in the Bristol Channel and up to full speed, we were amazed to find that there was no vibration whatsoever. The old ship had been smooth running, but the new one was practically silent!

From the very start, however, it was obvious that the workload was to be very high. As well as the heavy communication traffic dealing with the many teething troubles of the new ship, I also had to deal with the communication requirements of 132 passengers instead of the 76 of the old ship. The new equipment was very strange at first. All the main transmitters that I had sailed with previously were liberally covered in switches, buttons, meters and indicator lamps. The one I faced now was a completely blank steel cabinet, the only visible control being an on/off switch. It was controlled by a small keypad on the main console which was no bigger than a pocket calculator and very similar to look at. To select both transmit and receive frequencies, I simply had to key in a simple channel code and then press a button. For a few seconds, a series of whirrs and clicks would issue from the equipment and then when it stopped, I was ready to go. Although on the surface of it, you may think that this made things easier, I could foresee future problems when the whirring servo mechanisms did not actually do what they were supposed to. I also found it rather disconcerting that when I pressed the keypads, there was not even the slightest 'click' to indicate that the switch had actually made contact. As long as it worked, the job had become extremely simple and anyone aboard could have used it after reading the manuals for a few minutes.

The sound reproduction equipment was also in the radio office and, amongst other things, it contained four small tape players which could play music on a continuous loop. This 'musak' as it was called was churned out twenty-four hours a day to most decks and public rooms and was also available in all passenger cabins at the touch of a switch. I personally found this continuous drone of music especially annoying. A number of passengers also expressed similar feelings, so I took to only playing it at certain times and eventually leaving it off altogether. I was only ever asked to put it back on by the Hotel Services side of the ship who thought that it was a 'sign of professionalism'!

A lot of the old familiar faces had gone by then. Some had retired, others had moved on to other companies. Many of the officers who had made their first voyages in the old ship twelve years previously, had now reached senior positions. A minority of these were ever quick to point out that I was in a 'dead end' job and radio officers would soon be non essential and superfluous to requirements. Although I realised that this was true, it did not help to have it continually rubbed in, albeit in a jocular fashion. I wonder what they would have thought had they known that within ten years, their own jobs would be 'on the line' owing to the impending St Helena airport project whipping up the clouds of redundancy over the shipping service?

Another source of discontent was the food. On the old ship, the stated policy on food was simply for it to be good and uncomplicated. The food on the new ship, however, was fancy and complicated with exotic sauces and fancy dishes taking priority over the basics. While this appealed to a lot of people, it certainly did not appeal to me and I quickly found myself missing the old ship badly.

As the voyage progressed, technical problems continued to arise and I could scarcely go for more than half an hour during the day without my services being required somewhere. In addition to the teething troubles of the new ship, there were also other more annoying duties. It was decided that a number of public address loudspeakers, telephones, microphone points and numerous other things had been either left out or installed in what were now considered to be the wrong places. The electrical officer and myself were expected to correct and alter all these 'mistakes and omissions'. This did not go down well with me at all. My attitude was that the company had given everyone their say in what went where during the design and building of the ship. Most of the officers had stood by at the shipyard at various times and they had still managed to get it wrong!

It would not be fair to say that there were no good times on the new ship. The accommodation and public rooms offered much more physical comfort than the old ship. The wood-planked after deck and permanent swimming pool were a welcome luxury and reminiscent of the old Union-Castle liners.

I was not the only one suffering discontent. The company was now effectively manning two big ships, the new *St Helena* and also the old one, now sailing under the name *Avalon*. On my first voyage south, the purser was dismayed to find that he was being transferred to the *Avalon* when we reached Cape Town to relieve his opposite number who had sailed out with the ship. This sort of thing was uppermost in lots of our minds and we wondered who would be next. Reports from the *Avalon* were less than satisfactory. A lot of the officers' cabins had been converted into passenger cabins and the officers moved to less comfortable areas of the ship. Passenger numbers had fallen to very low levels and the whole project was on the point of failure. Within weeks of us sailing from Cardiff, the *Avalon* venture collapsed and the ship was laid up for sale. Eventually she was sold for further trading, but this also fell through and the *Avalon*, formerly *St Helena*, formerly *Northland Prince* in which I had spent the best years of my sea life, was scrapped in India.

I had not given any of my slide shows on the new ship and a quite a number of passengers who had sailed in the old ship commented on this and asked me why. I replied that owning to the heavy workload, I did not really have time. This, to a great extent was true, but a greater reason was that I was thoroughly fed up with the whole situation.

With the clouds of redundancy gathering, I again took stock of the situation. From a personal point of view it was not too bad. The investments that I had made years previously when I had been denied shares in Curnow Shipping in 1981 were doing exceedingly well and had quadrupled in value over the intervening decade and showed every signs of continuing to do so. Since getting married, plus the advent of the new ship, I had lost my enthusiasm. I longed for the days when life at sea had been less comfortable, less well paid, more isolated and far less stressful. My qualifications were outdated and useless for anything ashore, but that was my own fault. On the other hand, once I left electronics and communications, I did not want to take it up elsewhere anyway.

About the same time, I had seen a documentary on television about William Frederick Cody (Buffalo Bill). Although the Wild West seems a world away from ships and the sea, it nurtured an idea which had been growing in my mind for some time. Cody had been born about 100 years before me. He survived the American Civil war and lived an adventurous life on the plains for many years. Eventually, progress and technology (the railroads) destroyed his way of life. Instead of fading away in self pity and idleness, he formed his famous Wild West Circus. Although to many, he appeared as a 'flamboyant poser', he brought colour and enjoyment to untold thousands of people all over the world. He relived his youth with a vigour and enthusiasm that passed itself on to his audiences in an astounding manner. The very fact that times were changing made his success even greater: he was making a career out of nostalgia!

In a similar manner, the late Commander Alan Villiers had enjoyed a long and successful career as a writer, focusing on the final days of commercial sailing ships long after the ships themselves had passed away. Over the years, I had built up skills at building ship models and also studied the subject from a historical point of view. I was equally at home building sailing ships as well as the more modern types. That, I decided, was what I would do, I would become a full-time ship model builder and recreate the heyday of the Merchant Navy in miniature. Furthermore, I could never be replaced by encroaching technology—my course was set!

We had been advised that the management contract for the *St Helena* would be going out to tender in 1992. I therefore decided to remain at sea until that date. The reason for this was that if the contract was rescinded, we would, in all probability, be made redundant. Christine and I considered it worth hanging on until then to see what happened. In the meantime, I began building models in earnest while on leave and sounding out passengers on my models which were permanently displayed on the new ship.

About the time I joined the new ship, we received some significant tax concessions. Provided we spent at least six months out of the country per year, we became exempt from income tax. This resulted in quite a considerable pay rise which kept everyone happy for a while. The company took the opportunity to award us a small pay cut at the same time. Because this was more than cancelled out by the fact that we no longer had to pay income tax, it was accepted quietly, but it was a sign of 'things to come'.

My first voyage, apart from work and technical problems, passed without any major incident. My next voyage, which began on the 7th August included a major incident which I will now relate. When I joined the ship, I was pleased to find that my old friend Captain Bob Wyatt had returned from the *Avalon* to take command of the *St Helena*. The voyage went without any major problems until our arrival at St Helena. As we slowly approached the anchorage, the ship began to shake and vibrate, leaping backwards and forwards in a most alarming manner. The big double mast on top of the bridge was jerking to such an extent that we feared it might actually fall. Even from the shore, subsequent reports said that it was obvious that there was something seriously wrong. Down below, the engine temperatures were shooting up with no apparent reason and in due course both engines were shut down and the vibration ceased immediately. The anchor was dropped and our 4th engineer Fred Peters, a St Helenan officer and keen scuba diver was sent ashore to pick up his diving equipment. On his return, he went down to have a look at the propellers. In the crystal clear waters of the anchorage, the problem was immediately apparent. A large polypropylene fishing net had become entangled round one of the propellers. In the fading light, nothing was to be done that evening, so the ship settled down for the night.

The following morning Fred, wielding a huge knife, descended once more to cut the net free. On deck cargo work continued as normal. I was busy in the radio office with the usual unremitting communications when I was advised by the local radio station that the fishing vessel *Oman Sea One*, normally based at St Helena, was missing presumed sunk. Shortly before, the Panamanian oil tanker *Ruth M.* had come across two life rafts ninety miles north-west of St Helena. One of the life rafts contained nine men, while the second three. Among the survivors was the vessel's British chief officer Cyril Cudd. Five men were missing, including the captain. Mr Cudd said that at about 0600, he was off watch and asleep in his bunk. The ship was suddenly overwhelmed and within minutes he was fighting for his life as the sea poured in through the door. They were still unclear about what had actually happened and there had not been time to get a distress call out.

I immediately passed the news to Captain Wyatt. Governor Hoole then telephoned from the island to ask if the net had been freed from the propeller yet as he required us to put to sea as soon as possible to join in the search for the five missing men. Within a very short time, the net was freed and cargo work was temporarily suspended and we sailed at maximum speed towards the position where the *Oman Sea One* was supposed to have sunk. Shortly after sailing, we passed the *Ruth M.* which was on its way to St Helena with the survivors. I then made contact with an American aircraft which had left Ascension Island to help with the search. They advised us that the bow of the partly submerged fishing vessel was sticking vertically out of the water. We reached the scene and located the wreck shortly after 2200 hours that evening and quickly found the hulk. I was far too busy with communications to go out and take a look, but about twenty-five feet of the bow was standing vertically above the water when we arrived. There were no lights showing on the wreck and no signs of life. We combed the area throughout the night with searchlights playing on the water and the wreck, but no survivors were located. There was little we could do in the dark and the aircraft returned to Ascension Island after advising us that another one would be coming out to take its place in the next few hours. By this time, we had been joined by the Cypriot cargo vessel *Padrone* and they also patrolled throughout the night.

Very early the following morning, the replacement aircraft called us again. A grey dawn was beginning to break, but visibility was poor with rain and mist. Having spoken to the aircraft, I went out onto the bridge to report to Captain Wyatt that it had resumed the search. We were still circling the wreck searching for signs of life, but it had sunk so low in the water that only about a foot of it was above the water. Suddenly, and without any appreciable disturbance of water, it was gone, leaving only a thin film of oil on the surface of the sea. We turned for another sweep of the area. As we came round, I was looking out over the after starboard quarter with a pair of binoculars when I spotted something resembling a paint can floating in the patch of oil. I alerted Captain Wyatt who told me to keep it in sight and he brought the ship round. I walked slowly aft, round the back of the boat deck and onto the port side while carefully keeping the object in sight. As I was passing number two lifeboat, the 'object' suddenly sprang to life with frantically waving arms thrown up and faint cries echoing across the water. The order was immediately given to lower number two boat. Chief officer Bob Hone was in charge. In the front of the boat was 2nd officer Rodney Young; David Yon, 2nd engineer, was controlling the lifeboat's engine. A number of seamen were also in the boat. As it sped off across the sea, we could see it rising and falling on the heavy swells. To further complicate matters, we could see great lengths of rope, tangled nets and other debris snaking down into the crystal clear depths to the sinking *Oman Sea One*. There was a very real danger that they would get entangled round our propellers or stabilisers as the vessel sank and it was a very eerie sight. After a few minutes the boat, guided by instructions from the bridge of the *St Helena*, sighted the survivor and headed towards him. As it drew close, Rodney Young in the bows of the lifeboats took the megaphone and called to him 'Don't move. Stay where you are, you are safe!' When the incident was all over, this went down as one of the most classic statements ever uttered in the history of the company! With the survivor aboard the lifeboat, it sped back to the ship. The weather was deteriorating and it took several attempts to hook the lifeboat on to the falls and hoist it. At the boat deck, Dr Stevenson, ship's surgeon, was standing by and the survivor was rushed off to the ship's hospital. We continued to search the area for a further twenty-four hours, but no other survivors were found and we returned to St Helena. The survivor was the cook of the *Oman Sea One*. When the ship was overwhelmed, he was inside the forecastle. As the vessel upended, he was able to see out through a porthole and in view of the fact that the ship did not seem to be in imminent danger of sinking, he decided to remain there for the time being. When it grew dark, he was able to see the lights of the approaching *St Helena*, and later on, the searchlight playing on the wreck. He coolly considered his chances. If he got out during darkness, he might not be seen. All night long, he clung there in the dank forecastle awaiting the dawn. When it became sufficiently light and the *St Helena* approached again on a close-pass, he threw off the clips of the small hatch and scrambled out into the sea. The air trapped in the hull poured out through the new opening and within minutes the *Oman Sea One* was taking her final plunge. He had managed to get a lifejacket on and just lay in the water awaiting rescue. Once aboard the *St Helena*, he made a quick recovery, although he was reluctant to go out on deck for some time.

Three days later we sailed from St Helena towards Cape Town with seven of the survivors aboard. Of the seventeen crew members of *Oman Sea One*, thirteen survived. The captain, two engineers and one deckhand were lost. It had been a tiring and nail-biting time, but none of us begrudged it, and we had the personal satisfaction of rescuing one man after all hope had apparently gone. It was simply a case of the 'Brotherhood of the Sea', where no call for aid shall go unanswered. The remainder of the voyage passed without incident other than the now usual 'teething problems' which still persisted in all departments.

My next voyage, commencing on the 15th December, 1991, was to be my last Christmas at sea. Although no great dramas were enacted, the voyage was not without its troubles. A certain amount of discontent was beginning to show amongst the officers and crew as well as the passengers. As far as the ship's company were concerned, it was concerned with pay. As I have already mentioned, we were no longer paying income tax as we were normally spending more than six months out of the country. This had amounted, in effect, to a substantial pay rise. We were advised, however, that in order to secure a renewal of the management contract, our pay would have to be reduced drastically once the new management contract was secured. But as we did not pay income tax, we would really be no worse off than before the tax concessions. This was true of course, but it was the old story of give with one hand, take away with the other. I don't think any of us blamed the company. If the running costs were not reduced drastically, we would not get the new contract and that was the 'bottom line'.

More old faces had already left for various reasons and this had made for some promotions in the deck and engine departments, but, for the two radio officers, there was nowhere to be promoted to: we were in a 'dead end' job!

Some of the passengers on that voyage had been regulars on the old ship. They had enjoyed the experience so much, that they had persuaded a group of friends to join them on the new ship. Despite the increased comfort, however, they found that it did not have the relaxed intimacy of the old vessel, as it had not yet begun to develop any character. They were less than impressed by the fancy food, as were the majority of the passengers. As the voyage wore on, the complaints grew and finally Captain Wyatt ordered a return to the type of menu that we had enjoyed on the old ship. As soon as this was implemented, the complaints ceased.

As time passed, the technical problems began to wear me down and I longed for redundancy. By the time we reached Cape Town, I learned that both Captain Wyatt and Brian Cooper, chief engineer, were to take early retirement at the end of the voyage and I wished I were a bit older in order that I might do the same. The tenders for the new management contract went out and we were told that in due course we would all be made redundant and receive the redundancy payments to which we were entitled according to our length of time at sea. We would then be offered our jobs back under new 'terms and conditions'! At the end of the voyage, Captain Wyatt and Brian Cooper departed. One of our long-term 2nd engineers, Tim Walpole, had been made redundant the previous voyage, but he was recalled at short notice with the welcome news that he was to replace Brian as chief engineer. Another promotion went to chief officer Dave Roberts, who had started with the company twelve years previously as 3rd officer. He was to take command in place of Bob Wyatt.

On 18th April, 1991, Christine and I joined the ship for what was to be our last voyage together. Nothing untoward happened apart from the usual heavy work load and a suppressed feeling of discontent amongst the ship's company. The ship's company all continued to get on well enough with each other, but I suppose the worry and uncertainty of whether or not the management contract would be renewed was wearing us all down. With the British Merchant Navy in a definite decline, as well as our increasing ages, it was by no means certain that any of the more senior officers could find comparable employment in other companies.

When we arrived in Cardiff, a number of representatives of other shipping companies came aboard to inspect the ship and interview us as to the workings of it. We all answered the questions truthfully enough, but volunteered nothing and essentially only spoke in general terms or to reply guardedly to specific questions. At the end of that voyage Angie Read, 2nd purser, left the company. Angie had been with Curnow ever since the old *St Helena* first went on the run.

My final voyage began on 15th August, 1991. By this time, the teething troubles of the new ship were beginning to die down a bit and life was not so hectic. Captain Martin Smith was in command. We had a new chief officer, fresh from the Blue Star Line. Making his first voyage as chief engineer was Tim

Walpole. Also aboard was Dr Donald Brown, who had been surgeon with the company for a number of years and had served in the old *St Helena* and the *Centaur* as well as the new ship. Most of the officers on my final voyage were friends of long standing, I had sailed with a number of them on several Union-Castle ships between 1965 and 1976 and then more-or-less continually in Curnow Shipping. Surrounded by all these old friends, I anticipated a happy final voyage.

During my leave, I had built a model of the four-masted barque *Archibald Russell* and sent it off to Christie's London as a trial run for my new career. We sailed off into fine weather and as I anticipated, all went well. I made no secret that as soon as I received the promised redundancy pay at the end of the voyage, I was calling it a day and leaving. This was viewed with amused disbelief as I was by then regarded as a 'permanent fixture' who would never consider leaving the sea.

When we got down as far as Ascension Island, we were joined by a Lieutenant Commander Judy Setter, RN who was being sent on an 'acquaint voyage' in order to become familiar with the ways of the Merchant Navy. We had been told that she would be working with the pursers. On her arrival, she was given the pilot's cabin which lay opposite the radio office. After we sailed, she went down to the bureau, where she worked for a couple of days and then came stamping up the stair declaring that she was 'fed up' with it as she wanted something more challenging. Captain Smith asked if she would like to assist in the radio office and she jumped at the chance. We got on very well and she made herself very useful doing the numerous corrections to the Admiralty List of Radio Signals for me, a job that I loathed. I also found that with my new and attractive assistant we received quite a lot of social calls at the radio office from other officers. There was a lot of good-natured banter going on between us all and the voyage was much enlivened by her presence on the top deck.

An annoying incident happened the night before we arrived in Cape Town. I was awakened at about 0430 in the morning by a frantic banging on my door, accompanied by an excited gabbling. My door was not locked and I shouted for whoever it was to come in. The banging and babbling continued, so I got up, donned my dressing gown and opened the door. I was confronted by a male passenger aged about thirty in a very agitated state. Eyes staring and hair awry. He was shouting that the bridge was in darkness, there was no one there and the ship was heading for the rocks! I told him to calm down, adding that of course there was someone on the bridge. Also that it was always in darkness at night or the officer of the watch couldn't see out! He wouldn't accept this and continued to rant on. I then began to get annoyed and started along the alleyway towards the bridge stairs. By this time I was shouting at him that considering there were only three cabins in that alleyway, the first being the captain's, the second being the chief officer's and finally, furthest away, myself the radio officer. Our ranks were clearly displayed above the doors and I demanded to know why, if the ship was in such grave and imminent danger, was he calling the radio officer rather than the captain or chief officer. I went in through the bridge door into the dimly lit chartroom with my excited friend hot on my heels. As I pushed the curtain aside to go into the bridge, the chief officer appeared at the extremity of his bridge pacing. 'Look', I shouted at the passenger, 'that's the chief officer!' I then went stamping off back to bed leaving the chief officer to deal with him and explain that the lights of Cape Town were still miles away and we were not 'heading for the rocks'!

There was great amusement next morning at breakfast. Captain Smith said he heard the pair of us shouting all the way along the alleyway and up the bridge stairs. When I asked him why he hadn't come out, he said with a grin 'Well, you seemed to be dealing with the situation in a most satisfactory manner!' The chief officer then related how he had tolerated the fellow for some time, but finally asked him to leave the bridge after he had sat in the pilot's chair without so much as asking permission.

Our stay in Cape Town was especially pleasant for me. We had arrived without any repairs outstanding and my time was practically my own. One day, Captain Smith asked me if I would join him for lunch ashore. This seemed to be a good idea and off we went. Before lunch we had a couple of drinks in the Firemen's Arms, a well-known Merchant Navy drinking establishment. He then said that we were going to have lunch with some VIP or other. I was a little dismayed by this as I had looked forward to a relaxing lunch and not some public relations meeting where I would have to watch what I said. After all this time, I can't remember who we had lunch with, but it passed off OK and a good time was had by all.

Another day I went ashore with Dr Brown, Paul the chief officer and Judy Setter. We looked round the Waterfront, a new leisure area which had sprung up in what was once the old docks. We also called in at the Maritime Museum and generally had a pleasant afternoon. The following day, Tim, our newly promoted chief engineer and his fiancée, Jan, asked 3rd officer John Harrison and I if we would like to join them on a day out in a car they had hired for the Cape Town stay. We had a fantastic day out touring the Cape Peninsula and called in at the Cape Yacht Club on the way back. We were also shown round an American millionaire's private motor yacht which was lying at the marina. The next day, the whole thing was repeated and in the evening a group of us went out for a meal at one of the Waterfront restaurants. The following day we sailed for home.

On arrival at St Helena, it was time to check all the fire alarms and smoke detectors in officer, passenger and crew cabins as well as in all public rooms and

Captain Smith and the author

storerooms. This was a long drawn out task which I never looked forward to. It wasn't specifically my job, but as the fire alarm systems were in the radio office, it generally fell on me and whoever was prepared to assist. At the same time, one of the computer monitors in the engine room had begun to play up again. It had been looked at several times by shore service engineers and they had been unable to locate the fault. A new one was ordered for our return to the UK. The fault was intermittent, and Tim asked if I would take a look at it. It was disconnected and sent up to the radio office. This was the afternoon that I was scheduled to help test the alarms. Malcolm Simpson, the 2nd catering officer, undertook to do this job, working with the chief officer and Judy. As they went about testing the alarms, I worked quietly on the monitor and by late afternoon the testing had been completed and I had located and cured the fault on the monitor.

The voyage north passed off without incident. I made the most of enjoying sights, sounds and places that I was unlikely to see again. We encountered a bit of heavy weather in the Bay of Biscay, but it was not bad enough to make things uncomfortable. I had a bit of maintenance work to do on the forecastle head one afternoon and, although dressed in oilskins, got thoroughly soaked in spray. The weather was not cold and the job was not difficult, so I savoured my last taste of real sea air and spray.

We were scheduled for our annual dry-dock and had been booked in at Falmouth rather than Cardiff. I was not too happy about this as it almost doubled my train journey home. We were also advised that the management contract had again been awarded to Curnow Shipping. This news was met with general relief that jobs were safe, although the pay was to be reduced. On arrival morning, I took the radio log out on to the bridge for the captain's signature and as he signed he asked 'Well, is that really it then?' 'Yes,' I replied, 'that's really it!' I had a distinct feeling that he did not really believe it.

I remained on board through most of the dry-dock period as there was some work to do. My last job was withdrawing and cleaning the speed log probe which went through the hull at the bottom of number one hold. This was a dirty and uncomfortable procedure, but I was assisted by 2nd and 3rd officers Rodney Young and John Harrison. A few days later, the maritime sale at Christie's came up. I was pleased to learn that my model of the *Archibald Russell* had sold for a respectable £990! This gave me confidence for the future and I found that I was looking forward to my new career.

Before I left, there were a number of meetings held aboard concerning the new contract. We were told that although we had been enjoying a one voyage on, one voyage off leave ratio, our actual entitlement was two voyages on followed by one off. This was very true, but apart from the special circumstances such as the Falklands and the building of the new ship, most of the officers had been enjoying the voyage on, voyage off system since 1978. We were advised that our pay would remain the same, but we would only get one voyage off for every two served. Because the company was only managing one ship, this appeared to be impossible. The solution was, of course, for everyone to carry on doing one voyage on and one voyage off, but with a further pay cut to compensate. This pay cut was to be a further twenty-five per cent. So together with the five per cent cut of a few months ago, the overall cut was to be a massive thirty per cent! The union was called in and further meetings were held. The bottom line was that we had been enjoying extra leave for a number of years and now it was time to 'tighten the belt'. Nothing could be done and the company were well within their rights. It was also correctly pointed out that as we did not have to pay income tax, we had not really suffered any financial loss at all! Again quite true, but I personally did not feel like doing exactly the same job for a thirty per cent pay cut. The general attitude was 'If you can't stand the heat, get out of the kitchen'. Well, I couldn't stand the heat, so that was exactly what I was going to do. We were somewhat cheered when we learned that we would all receive redundancy pay and then would be offered our jobs back on the new terms.

I was not the only one to decide to leave. Neil, my opposite number, was to complete one further voyage before leaving for a shore job. Both electrical officers left, as did the 3rd officer and one catering officer. The remaining few days were quite enjoyable. The weather was good and I went ashore often, usually with Donald Brown, the ship's surgeon. I had accumulated quite a lot of luggage over the years and I decided to send this home as unaccompanied baggage, by Red Star.

On my final morning, a message came in from the company that one of our former passengers, Ronnie Eriksen, was just completing a book called *St Helena Lifeline*. He requested a photograph of Captain Smith and myself for inclusion in the book. I donned my uniform for the last time and the photographs were taken on the bridge. After that, I spent some time talking with the captain over the events of the past thirteen years. He still didn't seem to believe that I was going.

The following morning, I rose early and made my own breakfast in the pantry and then went down the lift to the gangway. Several of the crew had turned out to say goodbye. I walked along the quay pulling my wheeled suitcase behind me. It was the same one I had used when I joined my first ship 31 years before. At the end of the dry-dock, I looked back at the ship, but I did not feel any sadness such as I had felt when I last saw the old *St Helena*, just relief. No taxis were available and I walked slowly up the hill to Falmouth railway station. During the journey I experienced a splendid feeling of elation as all the stress of the past couple of years flowed out of me.

A few days after I arrived at home, the company telephoned to ask if I was coming back on the following trip. I told them that I was not, but there were no hard feelings, I had simply had enough.My new career of ship-modelling made a slow start initially, but after two lean years, it suddenly 'took off'. Private commissions poured in and we enjoy considerable successes at the Christie's maritime sales twice yearly. At the time of writing 208 models have been completed and, apart from half a dozen or so in our own permanent collection, all have sold.

I remained in contact with the company, mainly through Andrew Bell, the managing director. He was good enough to put quite a bit of modelling work our way in the early years, including a major repair to a professionally built model of the new *St Helena* which had been dropped in transport and seriously damaged.

With the new contract secured, Curnow Shipping continued to manage the new *St Helena* for a further nine years. The position of marine radio officer was abolished internationally about seven years later. All the British coast stations, including the famous Portishead Radio were closed down. The British Merchant Fleet had by then sunk to an all time low of less than 300 ships. What remained were mostly cruise liners, ferries and oil tankers. The old Merchant Navy has gone and I, for one, regret its passing.

In the year 2000 Andrew Bell, one of the founders of Curnow Shipping, stepped down as managing director. At that time the management contract was coming up for renewal. This contract, which Curnow Shipping had held since 1978, was rescinded in 2001 and awarded to Andrew Weir's Bank Line, a long-established company highly regarded in shipping circles for over a hundred years. Bank Line took on all the Curnow officers and crew who wished to remain with the ship. Of the originals, only Captain Martin Smith and Chief Engineer Tim Walpole remain. Curnow Shipping ceased to exist shortly after the rescinding of the *St Helena* management contract.

At the time of writing, the *St Helena* continues to serve the islands of St Helena and Ascension. However, plans are afoot to build an airfield on the island of St Helena. Once this is done, the shipping service, which has endured for well over a century, will be obsolete. Time, like an ever-rolling stream, bears all its sons away! As sailing ships gave way to steam and motor ships, so the modern motor liner will be forced to bow out of the St Helena mail service in favour of air travel, bringing another era to a close. The world will be a poorer place.

Photo Journal

The Bandama *at Port St Louis, a few days before I left to join RMS* St Helena

The liner RMS Windsor Castle *in which I first met many of the future officers of RMS* St Helena

Before the funnel was fitted, the ship had a very strange look

Frog racing

Dinner on deck

The ramshackle tour bus at St Helena *during the early years*

The boat deck is stripped on arrival at Avonmouth

The Aragonite

Officers and crew of RMS St Helena, *May 1982, Portsmouth*

Replenishing a minehunter at sea

Returning to RMS St Helena from HMS Ledbury in a rubber boat

Lt Newlands and Forward Support Unit

Bahia Buen Suceso *at San Carlos: the ship that started the war*

St Helena *officers aboard the* Bahia Buen Suceso, *San Carlos 1982*

The British field hospital at San Carlos

Enemy helicopter, Port Stanley

King Edward Cove, Grytviken

Rolling home on the final voyage

Some Facts about RMS *St Helena*

Between October 1977 and December 1990 the *St Helena* completed a total of 71 voyages under the management of Curnow Shipping. Voyages 1 to 25 were spent on the UK–St Helena–South Africa run carrying Royal Mail, passengers and cargo. Voyages 26, 27 and 28 were taken up by a Ministry of Defence charter, initially as a mine hunter support ship and latterly as a mini troop/supply ship. Voyages 29 to 71 were spent entirely on the UK–St Helena–South Africa service.

* * *

During the ship's life as the *St Helena*, she called at the following ports: Avonmouth, Tenerife, Las Palmas, Madeira, Cape Verde Islands, Ascension, St Helena, Cape Town, Tristan da Cunha, Port Stanley, San Carlos, Grytviken, Rosyth, Gibraltar, Teesport, Milford Haven, Cardiff, Newport, Southampton, Portsmouth, Portland, Falmouth, Penzance, Dakar, Simonstown, Vancouver, Panama Canal and Ponta Delgada.

* * *

Passengers from the following countries and islands were carried: St Helena, Great Britain, South Africa, Canada, Germany, United States of America, Paraguay, Japan, Austria, Australia, Korea, Denmark, Sweden, Finland, Norway, Mexico, France, Switzerland, Italy, Poland, India, Mauritius, New Zealand, Spain, Solomon Islands, Nepal, Portugal, Netherlands, Ireland, Kenya, Falkland Islands, Tristan da Cunha and Lichtenstein.

* * *

The total cargo carried was in the region of 49,000 tons and the ship sailed a distance of about 840,000 miles.

* * *

The following is an approximate list of the food consumed on board between 1978 and 1990:

Meat – 213 tons	Poultry – 43 tons
Fish – 41 tons	Potatoes – 190 tons
Vegetables – 160 tons	Ice cream – 51 tons
Sugar – 24 tons	Eggs – 518,400
Tea – 4 tons	Cheese – 21 tons
Milk – 113,616 litres	Coffee – 2 tons

* * *

The total number of passengers amounted to about 24,000 including royalty and titled persons.

* * *

During her twelve years as the *St Helena*, slightly over £15,000 was raised onboard for various charities connected with St Helena and the sea.

* * *

Animal passengers who travelled in the ship were:
sheep, rams, horses, cats, dogs, pigs, tortoises, parrots, bulls, gerbils, hamsters, hens, budgerigars, canaries, goats, peacocks, frogs, toads, cows and live eggs in incubators.

* * *

In 1990, the Stork diesel engine had run for a total number of 141,017 hours since the ship went into service as the *Northland Prince* in 1963.

* * *

The total fuel consumption since she became the *St Helena* in 1978 amounted to 38,009 tons (10,072,385 gallons). The lubricating oil used was 59,100 gallons and the cylinder oil 35,460 gallons.

* * *

At the end of that time, the engine still had its original pistons, liners and block!

* * *